KAIROS

LAURA KENNINGTON

Kairos
Copyright © 2019 Laura Kennington
All rights reserved.

First published in 2019.

Front cover photo by: Raphael Rychetsky

Edited by
Liz Marvin

ISBN: 978-1-9161557-2-5

Dedicated to my favourite mini explorers, my nieces and nephews: Izzie, Alex, Phoebe, Mia, Matilda and Freddy.

Here's to all the adventures ahead!

CONTENTS

KAIROS

Kairos: The right or opportune moment (the supreme moment); a time lapse, a moment of indeterminate time in which everything happens. The perfect, delicate, crucial moment; the fleeting rightness of time and place that creates the opportune atmosphere for action, words, or movement.

INTRODUCTION

'Now tell me, what is it you plan to do with your one wild and precious life?'
– Mary Oliver

I'm standing on the edge of a 40-foot cliff, surrounded by a glacial lake, getting ready to jump. There's snow on all sides of the water below, and it crunched under our boots as we steadily climbed up to the top of the cliff.

The sheer drop below is terrifying – littered with any number of rocks that I could hit on the way down. The slightest misstep and the result could be catastrophic. All the same, as I run through my internal risk assessment, I decide that if this doesn't work out then, all things considered, I'd be relieved that I wouldn't have to go back to the office next week. It seems like a win-win situation. I hate my job that much.

One, two, three . . . GO! Adrenaline surges through every fibre of my body. I run and the land disappears from under my feet but my legs – not getting the memo – carry on running at full speed through the air as we fall – much like the Road Runner cartoon. I immediately regret the decision to jump and, considering that these may well be my final moments, I also start to regret all the things I didn't get to do before my untimely demise until SMACK! We hit the water.

It is freezing cold and I have to fight furiously to get back to the surface. Eventually I make it. The icy water has taken my breath away and, although I am struggling to speak, I have the biggest grin plastered all over my face. We didn't hit the rocks, we have just jumped off a huge cliff into a bitterly cold lake in a stunt that would have fitted in perfectly to a blockbuster action movie and we are ALIVE.

Quickly, we focus on swimming to the shore, mindful of needing to keep moving to stay warm and to get out of the icy water as soon as possible. Clambering clumsily out of the water and up on to the gravelly bank I am shivering uncontrollably but I'm also euphoric and full of sheer, unadulterated joy.

It occurs to me that a few hours earlier, I was a different person – neither crazy nor brave – but this leap has changed everything and there will be no turning back.

IN THE MIDST of a mid-twenties life crisis, while working for an insurance company to save up for a mortgage that was someone else's dream and not mine – the same someone who has recently broken up with me – I put my corporate wages to good use and took myself to San Francisco for a bit of soul searching. It's the first time I've ever taken a trip by myself, but the life I knew had just been completely derailed and I needed to get myself back on track. I didn't even know what track that might be, but I knew I wouldn't find it by staying home.

Before succumbing to the pressure of a nine-to-five job, my background was in the arts industry – I went to a theatre school until I was 16 and after A-Levels, I'd skipped university all together. Instead, I went straight on to a Post-Graduate one year acting diploma. At age 19, I was the youngest on the course. In my early twenties, I was scraping by as a struggling actress. Slowly but surely, the pressure of being a responsible adult had crept in. I'd looked around at friends who had 'normal' jobs and envied the things they could buy, the experiences they could enjoy. I could rarely afford to go out for dinner and would often be working several different jobs, all of them fairly soul destroying and with very antisocial hours (call centre, flyering for clubs, bartending and door hostess for a sleazy nightclub in Covent Garden, to name a few). I qualified as a fitness instructor as a less depressing way of earning money, but even with this I'd struggled to find rent money to live with my very financially responsible quantity surveyor boyfriend. When he'd pointed out that, by being self-employed, I'd apparently made it so much harder for us to get a mortgage, I'd decided it was time for me to 'grow up'. It was time to be 'realistic' and choose a more acceptable career.

My best impression of growing up resulted in getting a job at a huge insurance brokerage firm in the city of London, where my miserable days were spent strategising as to how to do as little actual work as possible. It wasn't difficult to coast by. I worked in a gracious, jovial and kind-hearted team of eight – as long as I looked busy, they simply assumed I was doing work for at least one of them. Generally, I only had a couple hours of actual work to do each day.

I spent the rest of my time keeping up appearances – putting on my 'serious concentration face' whilst sneakily reading adventure blogs and daydreaming of being brave enough to perhaps cycle around the world or row across an ocean. If I wasn't escaping into other people's adventures, I was carrying around a folder to various sections of the huge office (because if you carry a folder around, everyone assumes you're doing something terribly important) and sneaking into empty meeting rooms to complain to my mum and to my friend Weeze, who were both very sympathetic but also keen to point out that they'd thought this lifestyle choice might cause me some difficulty. They'd warned me in advance of exactly the same frustration I was now regularly complaining about.

Knowing me well, they were right. Months before finding myself in this full-time role, I'd been covering reception for a very stuffy office near St James' Park in London. I was prepping the modern boardroom with frosted glass walls for a meeting, making sure to follow the long litany of instructions very carefully – placement of tea spoons, angles of the cup handles, distance of the side plates in relation to the biscuits all written down with absolutely no room for error. With 20 minutes to spare before anyone else arrived into the office, I decided to call Weeze and let her know my shiny new life plan: respectable permanent job, mortgage, weekend trips to Ikea, lots of new clothes and fancy couples dinners. Weeze regularly bridged the gap in our earnings, often generously treating me to dinner and to theatre shows when I couldn't afford to go. Not once did she complain but all the same, I was excited that soon I would be able to repay the favour. Much to my surprise, she was not at all in favour and greeted my plan with abject horror.

'Cacku,' (her nickname for me, that none of us can

really remember the origin of) she said gently, 'this isn't you. You don't want a mortgage. You HATE working in offices, they make you completely and utterly miserable.'

'Yeah, but I think it's got to be worth it. I'm so fed up of not having any money and actually this isn't so bad really,' I protested, adjusting the coffee pot to make sure it was facing the right way in relation to the sugar bowl.

'No. You'll hate it. You'll absolutely hate it.' She retorted. She then proceeded to quote emails I'd sent her only a few days before this conversation, listing all the many, many things I despised about working in offices – not least of all the actual office buildings themselves.

It was true, I found them inherently claustrophobic and would often daydream of staging an elaborate break out of the window, victoriously abseiling down to freedom – regardless of the restrictive pencil skirt I'd inevitably be wearing in order to adhere to strict corporate dress codes.

'Yes, but the mortgage . . .' I'd replied, desperately.

'So what about the mortgage? It's NOT worth the misery. I don't think you've really thought this through. This isn't a temporary cover situation, it's every day, five days a week, for months and for years – this is what you'll have to deal with. It's going to really, really suck! This isn't you – you're changing too much of yourself to fit in with him.'

Deep down I knew she was right, but I went ahead with the plan anyway. That conversation haunted me now. The relationship that had been the driving force behind all of this broke down before I'd even had my interview for my new adult-approved role. I'd gone ahead with it anyway, not really knowing what else to do.

During the interview, still a bit shell-shocked about the whole thing, I distinctly remember going off on a spirited –

and totally irrelevant – tangent about how inspired I was by Ed Stafford, who had recently walked the length of the Amazon. I'd also shown considerably more enthusiasm for the company's charity outreach program than my actual role. I was sure that I wouldn't get the job but they were a friendly team and I think they valued having someone who would fit in personality wise.

Months later, I'd often find myself staring at myself in the office bathroom mirrors – barely recognising the enervated woman in a respectable outfit staring back at me. Who even was I now? Here I was with everything I'd been told I should have and should want. In theory, life had never been so financially successful and I should have been at my happiest – in reality, although endeavouring to appear cheerful enough on the outside, I was desperately miserable. I'd dug myself into a pit of boredom and dissatisfaction that no amount of spending seemed to fix. I racked up credit card debt, buying myself a new dress or treating myself to a new cardigan every lunchtime, always to get admiring coos from the other girls in the office, who often had done the same. The office mailroom was mostly full of parcels of clothing ordered online by the women who worked there.

I knew something had to change. I had lost all spark from my life and, deep down, no matter how nice it was to go out for dinner and buy birthday presents without thinking twice about how to fund them, I couldn't escape the thought that life was too short to be this miserable. I felt like I'd been conned – nobody had told me that life as a successful adult was so . . . well, utterly stagnant.

One afternoon, whilst mindlessly googling for facts about work-based misery (not my most productive afternoon, but also probably not my least either!), I came across a 'Global State of the Workplace' study conducted by an

American consultancy company that revealed that only 17 per cent of people in the UK were actively engaged with their jobs. Another study conducted by a British research firm revealed that one in four people were unhappy in their jobs. Apparently, this quiet discontentment was just something that most adults learnt to live with. That same afternoon, I also came across a statistic that said, on average, we spend 13 years of our lives working.

The thought of sacrificing over a decade of my life to a job that made me so deeply unhappy seemed like such an unbearable waste of both time and potential. I didn't want to be one of those statistics. I had more to offer the world than this, didn't I? I wanted to believe there was a better way to contribute to the world than by just buying lots of stuff. People seemed to be on a conveyor belt mindlessly driven towards milestones – as a child, it was 'when I grow up' and then it became 'when I get married/have kids/settle down' and finally 'when I've paid off the mortgage and I'm able to retire'. But what then? Is that when it was finally OK to start living – really living – and not just existing? I didn't want to wait that long.

The more I thought about it, the more absurd it looked to me: work a full time job to pay for a house and so you can buy lots of stuff – you need the house to contain all the stuff and you can't leave the job because you have to pay for the house. In my mind, it was akin to a human hamster wheel. What a weird system! We all know rich people that are miserable and celebrities that have a seemingly perfect life materially can still suffer so greatly mentally.

For the first time in my adult life, I was financially very comfortable, but it hadn't made me as happy as I thought it would. Why, despite so much evidence to the contrary, were so many people convinced that more money was the answer? Why did most people seem so dismissive and careless with the infinitely more precious resource of time? So many of these unspoken rules and socially accepted norms embedded into western culture seemed completely insane to me. The only reasoning behind it that I could see was that most other people were doing it too – but still no one could really tell me a compelling reason why it was a good idea. It was like these ideas of appropriate adult behaviour had spread like a virus and everyone was infected – a dynamic referred to by academics as 'social contagion'. It even sounds like a virus! In his book *Sapiens: A Brief History of Humankind*, Yuval Noah Harari refers to this phenomenon as an 'imagined reality' that forms part of cultures everywhere: 'Unlike lying, an imagined reality is something that everyone believes in, and as long as this communal belief exists, the imagined reality exerts force in the world.'

I wish I'd come across both of those terms at the time; they might have made me feel better. As it was, I just felt like I was all at odds with the world and I frequently wondered if there was something wrong with my internal wiring. Why couldn't I just get on with it like everyone else? I sometimes envied the people who were content to work in an office and steadily follow their straightforward life plan. They seemed happy enough and I often wished I could settle into that life, too. However, no matter how hard I tried, I had to accept that this just wasn't working. Sticking with a job I disliked as a stepping stone to something better was one thing, accepting that I was destined to be perpetually miserable in the long term because that was just 'part of life' was another.

I often thought about a particular strip from Bill Watterson's classic Calvin and Hobbes comic. In one frame, Calvin, a child, is sat looking incredibly grumpy and totally fed up at his school desk. In the next frame – the one I often use in my talks now – this misery builds up, like a volcano of frustration, to such an unbearable point for Calvin that he erupts in exasperation, yelling out: 'WHAT ON EARTH AM I DOING IN HERE ON THIS BEAUTIFUL DAY?! THIS IS THE ONLY LIFE I'VE GOT!!' In the next frame, Calvin has upturned the desk and is running out of the classroom screaming. To this day, I have yet to find anything that portrays my feelings at working in an office more accurately than that cartoon.

And so I booked the San Francisco trip on a whim, in a desperate attempt to rediscover the happy, creative and optimistic person I used to be, as opposed to the jaded, unenthused, greyed out, financially successful but boring shell in a pencil skirt I'd become. August couldn't come soon enough.

After a ten-hour flight, I arrived into San Francisco just before midnight, and from the moment I stepped out from the airport into the characteristically foggy air, it felt like home. All at once, I felt my entire body heave a sigh of relief and the coil of discontentment that had been gripping me for months gently relax enough to let me know that this had undoubtedly been the right decision. Some places are special – with San Francisco, it was love at first sight and no city has since come close.

The next morning, I hired a bicycle to ride over the magnificent Golden Gate Bridge (something I did more than once – I really like bridges) and the excitement of this was only matched by my visit to the infamous (and adorable) sea lions that reside by Pier 39. Fuelled by coffee and pastries, I thoroughly explored the different districts on foot and shamelessly continued to tick off all of the touristy things for a couple of days.

After this, I decided I'd break away a little further. I booked myself onto an adventure tour of Yosemite National Park, buying a sleeping bag en route to the campsite. The sheer scale of Yosemite is phenomenal, and I'd never seen anything like it before. Dramatic mountains, towering trees, vast valleys, peaceful lakes warmed by the sun and thick snow in the higher regions – it was humbling to feel so very small and nourishing for the soul to be surrounded by so much space. Far away from the stuffy office attire and manicured appearance and liberated from phone signal and the noise of other people's opinions, I found myself coming back to life. My hair was messy, I was laughing and I felt free.

The tour guide was a burly all American rugged mountain man called Jordan, who I instantly had a crush on – I always did have a soft spot for American accents. When he wasn't guiding tours through the American wilderness, Jordan could be found surfing or snowboarding – no hint of a responsible financial mortgage plan in sight. From where I was standing, his life priorities seemed to make much more sense than mine. After a morning of swimming and diving off small boulders and ledges into natural rock pools, we'd all gone hiking.

When Jordan suggested a couple of hours into our group hike, half-joking, that the next jump into water should be off a 40-foot cliff in the distance I was keen to impress him and so I found myself blurting out 'YES! LET'S DO IT' before my brain had really had a chance to catch up with what was going on. Much to my horror, he agreed.

Although I made out with some confidence that I did

this sort of thing all the time and I was some kind of wild, reckless and adventurous water ninja, the truth was that I was petrified. The two of us found ourselves up at the ledge, staring down at the sheer drop below, the occasional rock crumbling away and tumbling down. The rest of the group had sensibly opted out and were waiting for us at the end of the lake.

'So, I actually haven't tested this one before,' Jordan said, smiling. That irresistibly cheeky smile was definitely the reason I was in this mess to begin with – smiles like that should come with a warning.

'Well, there's one way to find out, right? Gotta live life!' I replied over-confidently, inwardly having a mild panic attack. What had I gotten myself into?

'Yeah, man! Totally. I love that you're so up for it! This is so rad,' he replied, grinning. 'I mean, I have got to be the worst tour guide, ever – this is so dangerous!' He laughed.

My stomach flipped. Several times. I felt sick. I imagined my poor parents hearing the news that I'd voluntarily leapt to my doom in a spur of idiocy to impress a boy and I felt wracked with guilt.

'OK, we have to make sure we clear the rocks,' he continued, in a slightly more serious tone as he peered carefully over the edge. 'It'll be REALLY bad if we hit those on the way down. We should take a running jump and, like, you need to really, really go for it.'

'Yeah, OK. Don't hit those – got it, dude!' I laughed, nervously. I was beginning to shake and I realised that there was a distinct possibility that I might be about to vomit all over Jordan the hunky tour guide.

This was completely out of character. For the second time in recent history, I found myself asking 'Who the hell am I?' The key difference was, this time, I rather liked the answer. I liked the idea of being the type of girl who embraced life and leapt off cliffs, hand in hand with a ruggedly handsome and free-spirited American. Yes, sod the polite dinner parties and the mortgage plan – that girl sounded awesome, I'd want to be friends with her. Imagine the stories she'd have to tell!

Growing up on a farm in Bury St Edmunds, Suffolk, my early childhood had always been spent outdoors getting up to mischief with the family dog, a white Alsatian called Hobo. I'd return home, often covered in bruises and scrapes and mud, after a day of exploring the countryside. My teenage years had largely been spent listening to punk music and dreaming up audacious plans for the future. I thought of the rebellious teen I'd been – going through several different hair colours and, later, with the help of a friend, backcombing and waxing my hair into thick dread-locks (thankfully this phase was quite brief – it both looked ridiculous and smelt awful). I'd spent many of my school years feeling out of step, and as an adult, not much had changed. I considered that the fierce and formidable girl I once was would be horrified at the placid woman I'd become. What a waste. All of that inner spark had since been buried under layers of 'adulting'. On top of that cliff, I felt the spark of that mischievous and daring girl returning. Sweaty, dishevelled and excited – perhaps this wasn't what responsible adults did but I was beginning to feel more like myself than I had in years.

I chuckled to myself – the irony of working for the 'Risk Solutions' department of the insurance company was not lost on me. This was reckless, stupid and undeniably dangerous, but compared to the decision of wasting away in an office, it seemed like the most logical choice I'd made in a long time. A life without risks is safer but it is also predictable and dull. Who said life was even meant to be safe? I also realised that if I did get badly hurt, I would at least be entitled to some extra time off work as a result – a thought that instantly cheered me up. It was time to leap. It was the literal leap of faith that changed everything.

WHEN I RETURNED HOME from America I still didn't know what I wanted to do with my life, but I did know with absolute certainty that I couldn't spend the next few years of my life wasting away in an office, desperately waiting for Friday and feeling close to tears every Sunday as I felt the increasing gravitational pull of Monday filling me with a sense of impending doom. That wasn't living at all, no matter how many 'responsible adult' boxes it ticked. Saving up for a mortgage had been someone else's dream; I figured I should just start now by figuring out what my dream might look like. It began as a process of elimination.

One thing was for sure, I felt like my body needed to move. Physical activity has always made me feel better – I'd imagine my various frustrations and difficulties sweating out through my pores, like some kind of sweaty exorcism. I'd taught group fitness classes over the years as a flexible way of earning income in between other ad hoc jobs and always enjoyed those, so it seemed logical to go one step further and work full time in the fitness industry.

So whilst still working full time at the office, I qualified as a personal trainer. It is to the credit of my boss that he never once complained about me using the office printer to print out my entire personal training manual, or that I was sitting at my desk brazenly highlighting the pages and revising. In return, the team often came to me for free advice on nutrition and exercise, so I convinced myself it was a fair deal.

My boss admitted it wasn't a huge surprise when I handed in my notice – he'd always suspected I didn't have my sights on an a career in the insurance industry, but he said he was glad that I'd been with them for the time I had. It was further testament to my lovely team that, despite my often questionable work ethic, I was given a wonderful send off, with my generous boss also putting a tab behind the bar.

As I walked, slightly unsteadily after a few cocktails, towards the train station a couple of hours later, 'Scream' by Dizzee Rascal – one of the official songs for the 2012 London Olympics – was playing through my earphones, and the lyrics gave me goosebumps. 'Today's the greatest day of my life' – I really thought it was. I'd done it; I'd broken out of the rat race!

I BEGAN my new career in earnest, thinking of all the lives I could change and how fulfilling it would be. Shortly before leaving my job, I'd moved into a small one bedroom flat in Leigh-on-Sea in Essex and I'd completely romanticised my new idyllic life by the coast. I had visions of long, meandering walks along the seafront courtesy of my new flexible working hours and the sense of satisfaction I'd feel at the end of the day having empowered my clients to realise their goals. No more bosses, pointless meetings and long hours staring at the clock for me – I'd be gloriously steering my own ship from now on!

In reality, I had only exchanged one office for another and I quickly grew tired of the stuffy gym environment, too. My client list built up slowly, so I supplemented my income with some local waitressing work where, being in my early twenties, I was apparently the oldest employee by six years. I slowly grow more and more disheartened, not least of all because I had always been a clumsy waitress. When I was 18, I'd briefly worked as a cocktail waitress and I'd regularly struggled to squeeze through the gauntlet of drunk people with my tray of drinks intact.

A couple of years later I'd also ruined someone's marriage proposal in the swanky tea room of the prestigious Savoy hotel in London by spilling hot tea everywhere – in my defence, I remember those trays being quite heavy but the French waiter in charge of training me was livid and refused to work with me after that, so they'd quickly moved me upstairs to the reservations department instead. That actually turned out to be a stroke of luck because life was pretty cushty upstairs. I was given the title of 'Food and Beverage Coordinator' and I shared a private office with one other person, Richard Underwood – 'PA to the Director of Food and Beverage' – who would go on to become a dear friend. Working with Richard was infinitely more fun, and better paid, than waitressing – a fact I tried to hide whenever I walked past the French waiter, who no doubt would have been even angrier to discover that my clumsiness had effectively landed me a promotion.

Unfortunately, although many things may improve with age, my waitressing skills definitely hadn't: on one especially memorable night in the Leigh-on-Sea restaurant, I turned around quickly and accidentally sent a pizza flying off the plate and across the room – like a frisbee – on to the lap of a man celebrating his birthday. That incident was at least hilarious; I obviously apologised profusely but I would like to point out, for the record, that was actually his pizza – what were the chances?! Sadly, he didn't see the funny side

– he frowned at me for the rest of the night and I was also given a serious lecture on 'pizza safety' by one of the teenagers.

In the gym I seemed to spend more time cleaning gym equipment than anything else and, with a couple of exceptions, most of my clients only seemed to be interested in looking good for their upcoming binge drinking holidays to Ibiza. I couldn't help but think that training purely to look fitter on the beach while you get absolutely annihilated was a huge waste of body potential. It saddened me that many people considered their bodies to be mere ornaments, and not the phenomenal instruments of physical endeavour they have the potential to be.

With no one nearby who was keen to explore the limits of what the body can do, I found my curiosity turning inwards. I had reached the conclusion that although I'd escaped the claustrophobia of life in an office, this life wasn't quite the right fit either. Those same old questions continued to niggle away at me – I'm capable of so much more than this, aren't I? What am I making of this life? Is this it? The questions spiralled . . .

My thoughts kept returning to all the stories of daring adventures I'd read. I'd return home from a tiring shift in the local restaurant – smelling mostly of pizza, or from a frustrating shift in the local gym – smelling mostly of disinfectant – and stare at the tattered world map I'd stuck to my hallway wall. It was the only vaguely decorative item in the otherwise drafty and rather neglected flat. I'd spend hours wistfully looking at that map, tracking my fingers over the routes from all the adventure stories I'd read. In the midst of my misery, I picked up Sarah Outen's *A Dip in the Ocean* – an epic tale of Sarah's solo row across the Indian Ocean in the wake of her grief over the sudden loss of her father. In stormy winter weather, the windows of my room would viciously rattle and as I hugged my hot water bottle closer (with finances being much tighter now, I had to use the central heating sparingly) and I couldn't help but think of what it must have been like for Sarah to face furious storms in her tiny boat, helplessly tossed around by the indomitable force of the sea, mighty waves towering above and then crashing down. The thought both terrified and thrilled me. Could I take on an endurance challenge? Could I do something worth reading about? What if, instead of reading about other people's phenomenal stories, I went out and wrote my own?

My personal training qualification had taught me that the human body is incredibly efficient at adapting to the physical demands placed upon it. You've probably heard about exercise resulting in the release of 'feel good' endorphins – these trigger a positive feeling in the body similar to that of morphine! Amongst its many benefits, exercise is also known to improve self-esteem, reduce stress and improve sleep. But what about the more intensive side to this – what about athletes? What if, like me, you'd always assumed you just weren't really built for *extreme* exercise? Here is a (very brief) insight into how the human body responds to sustained physical effort.

Firstly, on a cardiovascular level, there is a significant growth and improvement in coronary (relating to the heart) blood flow, thus allowing a greater capacity for work. Increased stroke volume, resulting in a larger cardiac output of the heart which, in turn, facilitates a greater flow of blood to the working muscles.

Then, my favourite bit. The improved blood supply to the active muscles is matched by a greater ability of these muscles to extract and utilise oxygen from the blood. This results in maximised aerobic potential in muscle fibres. That phrase – maximised aerobic potential – had always stuck with me. The very definition of potential is 'having or showing the capacity to develop into something in the future.' With all the potential in the world, nothing develops without first taking action. The body simply adapted to its environment, for better or for worse.

Previous notions I'd had of myself not being 'athletic enough' or 'genetically just not the sporty type' really didn't fit with what I now knew for a fact: if you change the demands you make on it, you can change your body. How far could I push it? If other people could do these awe-inspiring things, could I? I knew I had at least one relevant trait that I hoped would help make up for whatever I might be lacking in athletic ability: stubbornness. Maybe I wouldn't ever be an Olympian, and perhaps I wouldn't ever be the fastest or the strongest, but couldn't I at least try to be the best version of me? It was a small spark that turned into fireworks – it was both terrifying and exciting, an intoxicating combination I hadn't felt since leaping off the cliff in Yosemite. I knew I had both more to give and more to learn – but I certainly wasn't doing either working out of a gym.

Everything has a cost. We are generally used to obsessing about the financial costs of things – but what of the cost of time? I figured I could always make more money and get another job, but I couldn't invent more time and the cost of wasting my precious time in a job I hated was a price I no longer wanted to pay. I still didn't know what adventure I actually wanted to go on but I had two basic requirements: it would need to be somewhere new and it would need to be big. I was hungry for a challenge and I was desperate to break out of the stale life that I'd somehow ended up with.

I quit both the restaurant and the gym and I moved back home with Mum – getting ready to relaunch my life for the third time aged 27. I dived into challenges, woefully underprepared but undoubtedly making up for it with plenty of enthusiasm.

On a whim, I borrowed my eldest brother's very heavy mountain bike to cycle 60 miles from London to Brighton with a few friends, having only cycled 20 very flat miles before. I had somehow missed the memo about padded shorts making the whole thing a lot more comfortable and was also blissfully ignorant about cleated cycling shoes, so I just cycled in my gym trainers. This actually came in quite handy when I had to get off and push the bike up Ditchling Beacon – a hill that's infamous to cyclists but one I'd never heard of. Helpfully appearing right at the end of the London to Brighton route, when your legs are likely to already be a bit knackered, it boasts an average gradient of 9 per cent and a maximum gradient of 16 per cent – by the time I'd crawled to the top, last of our group, I was completely done in. However, a friend soon thrust an ice cream cone into my hand, courtesy of the very well placed ice cream van at the top of the hill, and as I gazed down on the view of the South Downs with the sunshine brightly shining and my legs burning, I thought it could well have been the best ice cream I'd ever tasted.

A few weeks later, I invested in an entry level road bike with an aluminium frame. Now, at the risk of ruining any notions you might have of me being a hardened adventurer, I have a confession: I absolutely love Disney films. Accordingly, I proudly named my bike Dory after the fish from Disney's *Finding Nemo* – they are both blue and I figured that 'Just Keep Swimming' (or, in this case, 'Just Keep Cycling') would be a useful motto. Blissfully naive again, I decided to more than double my greatest ever distance without doing any relevant training and tackle the 'Dunwich Dynamo' – an overnight ride of 112 miles from London to the Suffolk coast.

Whatever weight advantages I'd gained by getting a much more suitable bike were completely eradicated when I loaded it up with two panniers full of mostly unnecessary stuff – including a large tupperware container of gnocchi and pesto (that I never did get through), a large and therefore incredibly heavy water bladder (it never occurred to me that I would be able to resupply en route) and, optimistically, a bathing suit, towel and a change of clothes. I think I could have survived for a full week with the contents of those panniers. Hilariously, I could barely lift my bike on to the train from Essex into London – which perhaps should have been my first indication I'd packed a tad excessively for a challenge lasting less than 24 hours – but ignorance is bliss.

The beauty of the Dunwich Dynamo is that it's not an officially organised ride and, as such, anything goes. People meet at a pub in London Fields and begin to disperse any time from 8–9pm. Every kind of cyclist takes part; there were colour coordinated, smug and terribly serious cycling clubs that would tear past in pelotons, there were bikes covered in fairy lights with their owners decked out in bright fancy dress and, my personal favourite, a man with two adorable cocker spaniels in a trailer behind him.

I definitely didn't win any speed records for that ride and I distinctly remember arriving onto Dunwich Beach feeling disgruntled with sleep deprivation and, if I'm honest, rather underwhelmed and disappointed by the grey and dismal scene that greeted us – the swimming costume stayed firmly packed away. For days after, I also couldn't walk properly, but after catching up on some rest, the brutal ride that I'd vowed had put me off endurance challenges for life took on a rosy afterglow. I knew I was hooked. I have since learnt that this selective memory is a key part of all my challenges – usually the most savage of times are the ones that get remembered most fondly from the comfort of home.

As luck would have it, a much bigger adventure opportunity popped up soon after I moved back home, too. A friend of mine needed crew to sail a boat from Sweden back to the UK at the end of August – would I be interested? I'd never been sailing before but that didn't seem particularly relevant, so I said yes immediately.

I spent ten days crewing on board Pangaea Exploration's 72-foot yacht *Sea Dragon* from Sweden back to the UK. We set off at 4am on a Saturday morning. Thick fog surrounded us as we left Stockholm; the sun was just still coming up and through the haze I could just make out the lights of houses on the shore as we passed. It was beautifully quiet and eerily still. As Stockholm slept, we slowly made our way out to open water.

Over the next few days, we settled into our watch patterns and life on board. As phone signalled disappeared, I felt life get ever so much simpler. It was wonderful and just like the relative isolation of Yosemite a couple of years before, I knew I had made the right decision in seeking out this quiet space from which to consider my next steps. It's actually been proven that the higher the levels of CO_2 (i.e. in a confined room/office), the more sharply your mental abilities decline. If you ever have important decisions to make, I recommend heading somewhere vast that allows you to really breathe in the planet. Big decisions require big space. Unfortunately, though, this thought-provoking and scenic bliss was relatively short lived.

By the time we were well underway in the Baltic, the sea was starting to get a little choppy—and with it, the boat more like a seesaw. Shanley, the first mate, and I began our midnight–4am shift in high spirits, singing and giggling along to the irritatingly catchy song 'There's a New Sound' by The Muppets (warning: if you ever listen to this song, it will be stuck in your head for months to come!). I went down below to complete the first log of the watch (writing down things like our current speed, heading and location) and sadly, when I returned to deck, it was to be violently sick. It was all I could do to clip myself back on to the safety harness in time before violently hurling.

The rest of the watch was an upsetting mix of admiring the pretty constellations in the clear, dark night sky—and throwing up some more. My next shift followed a similar pattern. The seas had gotten a little rougher and from the moment I got up the steps to the deck, I had remained hunched over to one side throwing up roughly every 20 minutes – largely through my mouth but also sometimes through my nose – for the next four hours. Any trace of food was long gone and I was helpless to stop my body from further depleting itself. This hideous cycle of vomit—shiver—vomit was not the kind of endurance I had in mind. When Eric, the captain, came to relieve us at the end of the shift, I was barely able to string a sentence together and my throat was painfully raw.

Another member of the crew, James, was called in to cover my shifts after this as I slept. Closing my eyes was the only way I seemed to get any relief from the torture. I hated not being able to contribute but I was completely wiped out. I ventured out only twice from my bunk in the following 24 hours, for less than five minutes each time, to go to the 'head' (toilet), where I desperately tried to wee as quickly as possible so I could then turn around and vomit again. In case even that proved too much, I was also given a sick basin to keep by my side – though thankfully, I never needed to use it. Eventually, incredibly dehydrated, I forced down some water and dry crackers until finally I upgraded to bread and, a couple of days later, after what felt like an eternity, I weakly made my return to deck

Sea sickness, in it's all encompassing brutality, has got to be one of the most unpleasant physical things we can endure as humans. For those of you that have never experienced it, it's akin to being thrown into a washing machine as you suffer with food poisoning. Although it's caused by a disturbance of the inner ear – effectively the brain struggles to reconcile the conflicting messages it receives about your position in space and the motion surrounding you – it assaults each and every one of your senses and leaves you completely depleted.

Annoyingly, after suffering with a bout of labyrinthitis when I was 23 years old, I was now rather more susceptible to motion sickness. Labyrinthitis causes swelling in a delicate structure in your inner ear and this results in extreme dizziness and vertigo, as well as sickness and other symptoms which can go on for weeks – or even months. At the worst of it I was unable to stand upright or move without the world spinning. Thankfully, although unpleasant, my viral infection passed after a couple of weeks, but retrospectively it now seemed like paradise compared to those hellish few days in the North Sea.

I've heard sailors say that there are two stages of sea sickness. During the first, you're worried you might die. In the second, you wish you would die just to be done with the whole ordeal. By the time we reached the German port of Kiel, I was getting close to the second. I'd also earned myself a new nickname of 'Chunder Dragon'. As hideous as sea sickness is, it usually quickly abates as soon as you reach land. Fortunately we had an overnight stay in Kiel harbour, and I spent the whole day wandering around the city eating everything in sight, mainly ice cream.

It was another early start to depart Kiel and although I still felt weary, the waters were calm and, once again, life on board *Sea Dragon* settled into a peaceful rhythm. I'd swapped watch teams and was now paired up with Megan, the 20-something-year-old deckhand and Tom, a gentle American soul in his sixties who had been sailing for most of his life (he also made the best French toast I've ever tasted). It was an unlikely pairing but it worked brilliantly. Tom took great care of Meg and me, keeping a steady supply of hot drinks coming on midnight watches. Meg (who was later given the charming moniker of 'Chavvy Knickers' after teaching the rest of the American crew some British slang) and I would dance around vigorously on deck to Dizzee Rascal playing from my phone to keep warm, the red lights from our head torches darting around into the pitch black around us. Survival at its best.

I'd swapped over to a different type of sea sickness medication and the sea was much calmer so thankfully my alter ego 'Chunder Dragon' wasn't seen for the rest of the trip and the cheerful girl that had boarded the boat in Sweden returned once more. All the same, Chunder Dragon became a source of great amusement for the rest of the trip – we'd all spend hours exaggerating the characteristics of this mythical creature as if we were passing on legendary ghost stories around a campfire: 'Rarely seen in daylight, the formidable Chunder Dragon lurks in the underbelly of the ship. Some say her bright orange vomit causes blindness and madness amongst men, some say her heart was lost to the sea years ago and, cursed to chunder for ever more, her almighty wrath can only be appeased by an offering of dry crackers.'

Captain Eric also woke me up a few times, most notably the first time for a 4am shift, by suddenly appearing next to my bunk and playing AC/DC's 'Thunderstruck' through his phone – replacing 'THUNDER' with 'CHUNDER' as he sang along to the opening lines. To this day, I can't hear that song without giggling.

The final few days were characterised by glassy waters, breathtaking sunsets across uninterrupted horizons and a feeling of happy contentment. There were never any arguments on board *Sea Dragon*. We were an eclectic bunch, but each of us clicked in to form a team rhythm, like the cogs of a wheel. By the time we approached Dover, I knew I was going to miss life on board. However, I'd also realised that the sailing life wasn't the right fit for me. I was missing movement and the satisfying ache that comes after a day of physical effort. From that point on, I knew that all of my adventures would be endurance based and I wanted to be my own engine. It was time to get back to work and make it happen.

1 HUSTLE, BABY! HUSTLE!

'The man on top of the mountain didn't fall there'
— Vince Lombardi

I knew whatever adventure I was going to undertake would need funding so I re-registered with my favourite temp agency. Over the years, I'd gotten to know one of the recruiters, Ian, very well indeed. Ian, from Essex, is marvellously boisterous and whenever I rang him up to let him know that I was once again on the lookout for work, we'd usually end up giggling on the phone for 20 minutes and gossiping about his outrageous holiday antics or weekend shenanigans before even beginning to discuss work options. I hated having to seek out office work but my regular chats with Ian, who would always answer the call with a reliably cheerful ''Ello treacle!', were at least always guaranteed to make me laugh.

I soon found myself copy typing doctor's notes for a private health clinic in London, often feeling immensely frustrated at the health status of the various corporate patients who could have probably cured most of their ailments by simply eating less sugar and exercising just a little more, or at all. It's a worldwide issue: statistics provided by the World Health Organisation reveal that globally, one in four adults aren't getting enough exercise, increasing their risk of cardiovascular disease, type 2 diabetes, dementia and cancer. Unsurprisingly, this trend is influencing the younger generation, too. The WHO also found that more than 80 per cent of the world's adolescent population is insufficiently physically active.

I appreciate that paid income, by necessity, takes up a large portion of life, but that our health and wellbeing often takes a backseat is something I find deeply unsettling. When did the very body we live in and cannot replace become such an afterthought? I often think of the quote by Indian philosopher Jiddu Krishnamurti: 'It is no measure of health to be well adjusted to a profoundly sick society.'

To raise funds as quickly as possible, in addition to the 40 hours I worked each week in the office, I continued to teach freelance fitness classes and I also hosted a pub quiz every Wednesday evening in East London. I also brought my food to work with me every day in a tupperware container – desperately saving money wherever I could.

My saviour during this exhausting time was Brazilian jiu-jitsu. Twice a week I trained at London Fight Factory, doing a double session on Tuesday evenings and a single on Thursday. Without fail, I showed up and trained as hard as I could each week. BJJ became my meditation, my headspace and my family – for those hours each week I thought of nothing else.

At first, my ego had a hard time submitting – or 'tapping out' (literally tapping on the mat to signal defeat) – to my opponent. Like so many other over-enthusiastic white belts, I first stepped on the mats feeling like I needed to prove a point. I was fairly strong, and in some cases stronger than the other girls I rolled with, but this didn't matter one bit when faced with better technique. To start with I hated it. It would enrage me and I'd begin the next sparring session all the more determined that I wouldn't be caught out a second time. But, inevitably, I would have to tap out again, and again, and again. My ego had to learn to accept defeat.

The hours on the mat taught me discipline and humility, in no small way aided by the formidable head coach, a fiery Brazilian man called Luiz Ribiero, who would scream full volume at us should he ever consider our motivation to be lacking in the slightest. One hundred per cent – that was the deal. Ultimately, he was tough but always fair and those blue gym mats were a sanctuary to me. There was no room for egos in that basement and we all knew it. It's part of what made it so special.

BJJ is often described as a game of human chess – I couldn't blag my way out of it through strength, only time and diligent practice would help. This proved one of my most valuable lessons from my time at LFF. I promised myself only that I wouldn't give up just because I was tired, but I learnt to see the times I did have to tap out as learning opportunities, not rage-inducing failures. There were no shortcuts and I think the same is true for anything worth having. Life's best victories are earned. I get beaten up and humbled; I felt frustrated and triumphant; I left shattered but smiling.

No matter how tired I was – and often I was so tired I had to take a nap in the disabled toilet of the office during my lunch break – I never missed a session. It was a gruelling schedule but I focussed on working hard enough to squirrel away enough money that I could go on an adventure.

———

IF YOU'RE REALLY LOOKING for an adventure, it turns out that inspiration can be found anywhere. Mine found me in that East London pub on a cold and wet Wednesday September night, in the form of a pub quiz question.

'At double the length of the Danube, what is Europe's longest river?'

As I read this question aloud, I thought to myself, 'What a great setting for an adventure. I wonder if anyone has ever kayaked that river . . . I wonder if it's possible?' It didn't seem at all relevant that I had done very little paddling.

I got home that night at 11pm, with a 6am alarm waiting for me. Though I was usually in a rush to get into bed and get as much sleep as I could, I sat and googled that river to within an inch of its life. By the time I'd brushed my teeth and climbed wearily to bed, I had my adventure idea. I decided I was going to kayak the length of the Volga River in Russia – all 2,300 miles of it. It seemed very important to me to make it official by giving this monumental project a title before sleeping – it definitely couldn't wait. The river ended in the Caspian Sea, so before went to bed I named the endeavour 'The Caspian Challenge'. I eventually fell asleep at 1am, with a huge grin on my face. It was perfect.

Initial research told me the best time of year to go was May. That meant from first hearing about the river to getting to the start line, I would have nine months to pull it all together. The list of kit I needed to source seemed to breed on a daily basis. I captured it all on an immense spreadsheet: waterproof paddling jacket and trousers, a kayak trolley to make portaging all nine of the dams on the route possible, a PFD (personal flotation device), a camping stove to cook food and hundreds of ad hoc items in between. Oh, and I also needed a kayak and some paddles. I'd only been in a kayak twice but despite my woeful lack of experience in this area, it all seemed reasonable . . . ish.

I began to steadily work through the formidable kit list, still maintaining multiple jobs and weekly training sessions. A friend of mine, Jon Beardmore, was one of the first people I confided in about my idea and, with his help, the list became split into manageable categories and started to take shape.

Jon, who had recently returned from a 30,000-mile overlanding trip, driving through Central Asia, is a project manager in between his adventures. If there was ever anyone who could help keep me and my many lists on track, it was Jon. Being from New Zealand, he also had a really reassuring catch phrase that he'd often roll out whenever I started to feel overwhelmed: 'She'll be right.' No matter what was going on, this was usually Jon's response. Simple, but effective. It's a mantra I've since adopted.

I got some more information on the river itself from people who had paddled it before. Mark Kalch and West Hansen had kayaked it separately the year before and were so generous with answering the many, many questions I fired across them via email.

I began to piece together the logistics bit by bit, soaking up every scrap of information I could find on this mighty river. I marked the dams on my map, noting which side I'd need to be on to portage. I made notes of which sections of the river were especially wide and surrounded by high land – I'd need to ensure I had good weather for these sections as I wouldn't be able to bail if I needed to and wide rivers in bad conditions become sea-like with large waves. Being relatively new to paddling, I was more than happy to be over cautious in this respect, rather than to find myself in conditions I wasn't experienced enough to handle

I wrote to brands, pitching them the idea, to try and bring some of the costs down. Some companies offered me kit in return for exposure via social media and the promise of further exposure through public talks when I returned. I had little social media presence to speak of then, but I was working hard to build it up – approaching magazines, volunteering at adventure festivals and speaking to anyone and everyone I thought might be able to help.

A few months into starting the relentless hustle for the Caspian Challenge, my boldness was rewarded. I managed to partner up with KEEN, an American footwear company, and BAM Bamboo Clothing – a UK company who, as the name would suggest, make all their brilliant clothing from bamboo. MSR sponsored me with a stove and I also gained support from Venture Kayaks, who provided me with a gorgeous orange sea kayak and Ainsworth Paddles, who provided me with sleek carbon paddles. I became a proud ambassador for Aethic – whose ground-breaking and patented eco-compatible sunscreen guaranteed not to damage marine life as well as protect my skin. My friend Jon "She'll be Right" Beardmore also leant me a tracking device that would update a map with my location every few minutes, allowing people back home to follow my progress - much to my mum's relief, it also had an emergency SOS button.

The Russian Language Centre in London also kindly agreed to sponsor me for a beginner's course in Russian and also helped me translate a letter of introduction – the idea being that I could show this to people I met on the river and it would very quickly explain what I was doing, in a way that my basic Russian wouldn't be able to. Real Russia came on board with sorting out the necessary 3 month visa – a logistical feat in itself.

Although there were literally hundreds of 'no's', I tried to not let them bother me. Instead I focussed on each and every 'yes'. These were fuel to me: another person that believed enough in me to support the challenge, another cog in the wheel, another member of the team. Alongside the official brand partnerships, friends and family rallied around to support, generously donating their time and expertise.

I don't actually have a driving license so I relied on my friend Ed Underwood to take a day off work so we could take a very long road trip from Essex to Runcorn and back, 450 miles in total, to collect my kayak from the Venture factory. Days before, Ed and his dad Rob, both yacht brokers by trade, had actually built a custom roof rack from scratch especially for the occasion. Perhaps most impressively, Ed also managed to put up with my eclectic road trip playlist (featuring songs from musicals, gangster rap and, of course, power ballads from the 1980s) and accompanying car-karaoke for well over nine hours without once kicking me out or leaving me at a petrol station.

Thousands of small but wonderful gestures just like this built up, and knowing that, although this was a solo challenge, I was by no means alone kept me going through the long, hard slog to the start line. As another coping strategy for the time I was going to be spending alone, I gained an adventure mascot – a small green bear I named Murphy (naturally, being green, I determined that he was Irish). I also decided that the kayak would need a name – after all, she was a vital member of the team, too! Following, as ever, the Disney theme, it only seemed appropriate to name the kayak Merida, after the feisty orange haired heroine from Disney's *Brave*. I hoped it would remind me when I needed a little extra courage of my own.

The weekday schedule remained the same – Monday to Friday in the office, Tuesday and Thursday evenings at London Fight Factory and Wednesday evenings hosting the pub quiz. My social life became largely non-existent, but I didn't mind because I'd been captured by a purpose. London Fight Factory was a family in itself and they kept me sane.

I'd decided to raise money for a remarkable charity, Hope and Homes for Children, through the challenge. Hope and Homes for Children is a British-based charity but they work across seven different countries and their aim is to get children out of orphanages and into loving families. I'd decided to raise money for them because I was so very grateful for my own family – the one I'd been born into and also my 'adopted family' of close friends that had formed over the years. Rallying behind me, the gym started selling t-shirts to help me reach my fundraising targets and every penny raised helped to keep me motivated. It felt good to think that I might be making a difference, no matter how small. My jiu-jitsu team-mate, Borja, gave me a journal in a hand-crafted leather pouch – that he had made from scratch – to take with me. I was also given a fabric patch with the gym logo to take, too. There was a lot of love in that gym, woven in amidst all the sweat. And a poster of Mohammed Ali in the ladies changing room always reminded me the virtue of hard work. 'The fight is won or lost far away from witnesses – behind the lines, in the gym, and out there on the road, long before I dance under those lights' is one of many Ali quotes I'd read that had stuck with me. I figured that whenever things got tough and the cheesy Ali quotes weren't quite cutting it, I'd just picture Luiz furiously yelling at me and that would soon give me ample motivation to carry on.

The weekends were now full of more training. On Sunday mornings I completed a home-based strength and conditioning training session with kettlebells – I'd qualified as a kettlebell instructor a couple of years beforehand. And of course I went paddling whenever possible. A family friend, John Griffin, usefully happened to be a kayaking instructor based at an activity centre near my mum's house. In fact, there weren't many outdoor sports that John wasn't an instructor of. Generously, he'd spend most Saturday mornings – usually his day off – trying to teach me how to paddle more efficiently.

It was winter when we started and we'd often sit there with the elements howling around us – rain pelting down, lips gradually turning blue. But he never once complained and always kept me laughing. Often we would both be laughing at my poor technique. I'd perfected what I'd call a 'handbrake turn' in the water – rather than managing to paddle in a straight line, I'd suddenly have to aggressively dip the paddle in on the opposite side and turn it backwards, losing all momentum in the process, to swivel myself around and straighten out. We'd always find it funny but John would often gently remind me that it was going to be a very long 2,300 miles if I needed to do this regularly. He had a point.

The months rolled by and, despite the gruelling schedule, I remained determined and focussed. I told myself that the exhausting routine was all part of building up the endurance I'd need to handle three months alone on the river. For every sponsor that said no, I approached five more.

Just two months before my scheduled start date, with things coming nicely together, I ran into the biggest curve ball yet. This one threatened to derail the whole trip immediately.

It turned out that attempting to ship a sea kayak to Russia was a recipe for a really bad time. No matter how many companies I spoke to, the conclusion was always the same—flying it wouldn't be an option and the cost of sea freighting it would be three x the cost of the kayak itself—and the expense potentially wouldn't even stop there due to import charges. Road freight also came with the bonus prize of potential theft due to reported corruption along the route. Both Venture and I investigated a Plan B of using a kayak already out in Russia, but this also proved unsuccessful. With time running out until my scheduled departure, it seemed uniquely frustrating and a bit ridiculous to have everything else now lined up beautifully for Russia . . . Except for the kayak in the kayak challenge.

This would have been a total disaster had I not seen a film called *Nobody's River* a couple of months earlier. *Nobody's River* is a gorgeous film about four girls who set out to kayak down the Amur River from Mongolia to Russia. I immediately loved this film for many reasons but what was especially fortuitous about seeing it, was the type of kayak they used for their journey.

They each had a TRAK fold up kayak which, until the film, I'd never even heard of. Their 16-foot folding kayaks, large enough to hold all of their supplies (including filming gear, food, camping gear and clothes!), simply folded down into a bag roughly the size of a golf bag—meaning they were perfect for travelling to pretty much anywhere you needed as they could be checked in to a flight and even taken onto a train!

I'd had these clever Transformer-esque kayaks in my

head as the shipping issues continued to persist. Finally reaching a dead end with transporting my beloved Merida, I decided to see if this Canadian based company might be able to help. It was a long shot and I wasn't feeling especially confident as I knew I wasn't giving them very much notice at all and, at the very least, to ship a single kayak from Canada to the UK might prove expensive. Nonetheless, if you don't at least try you'll never know, right?

Having miscalculated the time difference in my slightly nervous excitement, I rang before they were even open for business. Luckily, the founder and managing director, Nolin Veillard, answered the phone and kindly let me explain the reason for my call all the same. I think it's forever to the credit of Nolin for being so open minded and for not dismissing my proposal straight away. Whilst he promised to investigate what, if anything, TRAK might be able to do, Nolin directed me to the TRAK files on YouTube, so I could find out a bit more about the specifics behind set up of the kayaks. Since first seeing them in *Nobody's River*, I'd actually heard quite a few great things about these kayaks but the TRAK files really sealed the deal; the more I learnt, the more I anxiously hoped that TRAK would somehow find a way to get involved with the Caspian Challenge.

Two weeks later, after a lot of hectic work behind the scenes at TRAK HQ, I was once again on the phone to Nolin for an update—fingers (and toes!) firmly crossed. I held my breath as he revealed that, against all odds, TRAK had somehow found me a kayak! Not only that, but they would be sending it over with one of their TRAK Pilots, Paul Diener, to help me get used to it. Paul is an ACA Level three Coastal Kayaking instructor and leads tours and expeditions in the Amazon rain forest with his TRAK kayaks, so

I would be in excellent hands. As if that wasn't magical enough, my kayak would also be in the colour I'd casually said would be my colour preference—red.

Remarkable moments like this define adventures and I still feel extremely grateful for the support of Nolin and his awesome team. After that, Nolin of TRAK Kayaks was referred to as Saint Nolin. I still get overwhelmed when I think of the magic of this Canadian company taking a chance on me. Years later, I'm very proud to be one of their TRAK Pilots. Without their initial support, I honestly don't know what I would have done. Sticking with the Disney theme, I named the kayak Ariel (from *The Little Mermaid*, naturally).

I now had two weeks to get used to assembling, paddling and packing her before we boarded a flight to Russia.

2 IT IS NOT THE CRITIC WHO COUNTS

'It is not the critic who counts; not the man who points out how the strong man stumbles, or where the doer of deeds could have done them better. The credit belongs to the man who is actually in the arena...'
– Theodore Roosevelt

I am at the airport waiting to board my flight to Moscow and I am torn between wanting to vomit and burst into tears. Despite being a 28 year old adult, it was emotional saying goodbye to Mum. Although I've spent months confidently preparing for this incredible voyage, I'm absolutely petrified. Without lists to keep me busy, my head fills with thousands of worse-case scenarios – most of them with a perfectly reasonable solution, whilst the others are just totally illogical and absurd. At the heart of all of them, I suppose, is a fear of failure. A fear that I have taken on something I'm not capable of pulling off and – worst of all – that I'm about to let a lot of people down. Diving in full throttle and figure it out later is very much how I operate, but I'm beginning to think I'm an idiot.

Having arranged to stay with a couple in Moscow via the website Couchsurfing.com, my worries immediately melt away thanks to their warm hospitality. Anton meets me at the airport and helps me load my gear into a taxi and then into the house, while Natasha cooks us all a hearty meal. Immediately, I have two new friends who set about helping me as much as they can with the few bits of admin I have to do before heading to the start of the river. Having Anton with me makes simple but taxing in a foreign language tasks like getting a sim card that much easier.

I also need to find a way to get to the source of the river – an eight-hour drive from Moscow. Anton and Natasha are excited about my challenge, and they wonder if any of their contacts might be able to help me along the journey. They put a message on Anton's social media profile on VK.com, a Russian social media networking site and the second most popular website in Russia. The message simply details what I'm doing, with links to my social media pages, and suggests that if anyone lives nearby on the route and can offer me a hot meal, a shower or a bed/couch for the night, that it would be gratefully received! None of us have any way of knowing the impact this simple, innocent gesture will have. The post immediately starts to buzz around the internet – I am sorting through my kit in the next room whilst Anton excitedly updates me on the incredible response.

'It's been shared 200 times!'

'It's had 40 comments already!'

By the time I go to bed that night, a couple of hours later, my own Facebook page has gained over 500 new fans and my inbox has been inundated with over 200 messages. I am overwhelmed and deeply humbled by this phenomenal welcome to Russia. Someone upstairs must really like me, I think. This is magical!

The social media numbers continue to explode. Anton's post has now gone totally viral – a phenomena that I had previously thought was limited to amusing cat videos on the internet. Amidst the hundred of messages I receive are many kind offers of a lift to the start of the river and I find myself in the totally unexpected position of being spoilt for choice.

Despite only having been in Moscow for two days, any preconceived notions of Russia I might have had have been obliterated before I've even started paddling. I thank everyone for their support and explain I can't physically respond to all of the messages but will endeavour to catch up as the journey continues.

I end up arranging to meet a lady called Elvira for the trip to the source of the river. She turns up armed with a gigantic flask of tea, a warm smile and an adorable collie dog called Tao. Within ten minutes of being on the road, it feels like we are two old friends on a road trip rather than two strangers catapulted together by odd circumstances and we giggle our way to Volgoverkhovye. The trip takes over nine hours and the closer we get to the source, the bumpier the road becomes. I feel quite relieved that I'm kayaking and not cycling.

With the sudden boom on social media, the press has also picked up on the story. I've agreed to meet a news crew to film a pre-trip interview by the bank of the river the next morning, delaying the start of my challenge for a day. It all feels totally surreal but I hope that all of this added publicity will boost donations to the charity, Hope and Homes for Children.

In all the excitement, I realised I have overlooked one of

the most basic things from my kit list; I have forgotten to pick up a lighter and don't have any matches with me. My clever MSR camping stove is useless without a way to light it and the accompanying gas canisters I'm carrying also totally redundant. So I ask the crew to bring a lighter with them. When they do arrive, I'm offered seven of them. Problem solved!

They have also brought three different presenters as the feature is to be translated into Spanish, Arabic and English, as well as Russian. I do my best to sound confident throughout the interviews:

'This is the biggest challenge I've done so far,' I say, subtly implying that I have perhaps done other similar challenges before, just not on this scale. It's not strictly a lie, but I consider that it could well be the understatement of the century.

It's a relief when everyone leaves. Between the immense social media publicity and the press, the pressure has been intense and I'm feeling completely overwhelmed. In the 72 hours since arriving into Russia, my Facebook page has now gained over 5,000 new fans and I have been sent well over 2,000 messages. My head is a whirlpool of anxious thoughts swirling around but, exhausted from the past few days, I fall asleep at 5pm.

An hour later, I'm woken up by a Russian man, saying something I don't understand with great enthusiasm outside of my tent. I instantly assume I'm camping somewhere I shouldn't be and that I'm about to get into trouble. I nervously scramble for my letter from the Russian Language Centre that explains what I am doing and groggily unzip my tent door.

I'm greeted by the warm smiling face of a fisherman. Seeming amused at the formality of my letter, he dismisses it and says he knows who I am because he has seen me on the news – he has simply brought me some firewood so I can make a fire. He is camping further down the lake and says if there is anything I need, I must let him know. He wishes me luck on my journey and then he is gone.

The next morning, after a broken night of sleep, everything takes longer than it should to pack up. I also discover that the 2.5kg of highly nutritious powdered breakfast smoothie mix I'd packed with me is fairly useless because I'm unable to squeeze enough water out of my Water To Go bottle, that filters the water to make it safe to drink. The only way to get the water through the filter is to suck it through the straw. Accordingly, my very first breakfast on the river involves me sucking the filtered water out of the bottle and then dribbling it into my cup, so I can make a thick, grainy paste out of the powder – which, incidentally, is bright green and effectively tastes like fruity cement.

After forcing myself to finish off the dubious breakfast, I wrestle everything into waterproof bags and cram them into Ariel, whilst thinking that I don't remember it being this difficult to fit everything in before. Truthfully, with the kayak only arriving two weeks before, this side of the prep had been a little rushed. Nevertheless, already covered in sweat from the effort of packing up, Ariel and I are on our way. Months of preparation has led to this one single moment. This is it. I turn on my tracking device and I take a big, triumphant breath in . . . only to burst into tears seconds later. The accumulated pressure all comes rushing out.

The first morning of the mighty Caspian Challenge is full of tears. I cry at how long it has taken me to pack up, I cry at the thought of eating grainy powder paste for the next two-and-a-half months and I cry at the overwhelming distance ahead of me. I then cry some more when I realise I had somehow set off in the wrong direction – which I only realise when I see the end of a lake where I should be seeing the rest of the river.

Once paddling, this time in the right direction, I start to feel better. The water is calm and I make good progress. Action is the best cure for nerves that I know. With every paddle stroke, I feel my confidence growing and my nerves subsiding. By the time I find my camp spot for the night, I am exhausted. I select a beach and settle in for the night, feeling irrationally intimidated and scared.

A wasp finds its way into the space between the inner and outer section of my tent and angrily buzzes away – this small annoyance sets off yet more tears. I lie in my sleeping bag on high alert; I hear distant voices and convince myself that they are smugglers of some kind. At best, smuggling drugs and at worst, trafficking people into slavery. I then go on to convince myself that if the water levels rise, the kayak could wash away as I sleep. Or that the voices I hear are actually plotting to steal things from my kayak before then coming to my tent to rob the contents of that, too. There is no basis for any of this but having not slept properly for nearly a week, I'm feeling a bit frazzled. Every word of caution, every warning of how unsafe it is for women to travel by themselves, sneaks its way in and invades my brain, no matter how much I protest and try to rationalise against it. Eventually, though, I'm so tired that I stop caring. I decide that if I am to be robbed tonight, I will at least have a nap first. I end up sleeping straight through the night. The soft sand makes for a very comfy bed.

The next day, I once again take an obscenely long time to pack up. I am aching all over – my body is not yet used to the demands of paddling all day. Once again, I feel overwhelmed at the vast distance before me and all of the unknown things it contains. I set off, cutting through the glassy still water as the heat bears down, with no breeze in sight. I take to filling my cap up with water from the river and pouring it over my head at regular intervals to cool myself down. Onwards I go, my paddle cutting through the dead flies that lie on the top of the water. As the afternoon approaches evening, I am eager to find a camp spot. The only bits of ground I come across are too conspicuous and I feel nervous of being so exposed. So I paddle on. And on. And on.

After two hours of extra paddling, I begin to deeply regret my decision to leave the potential camping ground earlier in the day. Foolishly, my headtorch is packed away in the rear of my kayak. There is high grass on the nearest bank making it impossible to get to land and I start to feel rising panic that I will be in deep trouble soon. I am exhausted and each paddle stroke takes all of my will. On and on it goes. I feel ridiculous and stupid: once again, the voice of every critic invades my head against my will and I begin to think they are right. I half-cry – too tired and dehydrated to actually cry – and silently pray for some kind of miracle whilst humming Aretha Franklin to myself in an attempt to keep my spirits up. Aretha doesn't really help, but a miracle, however, is exactly what I get.

Mikael Farikh is a helicopter pilot and he has been following my tracker. He has come to say hello. At first, I think I am hallucinating when I see a friendly helicopter pilot waving at me from the sky – have I finally cracked under the pressure of the last few weeks? There is flat, accessible land where Mikael lands his helicopter and, paddling over to meet him, I'm close to tears again – the sheer relief to be on land again is overpowering. As if this bizarre situation wasn't quite incredible enough, Mikael has also brought what he deems to be all the essential supplies I could need: insect repellant, orange slices, a mosquito hat, some chocolates and a bottle of Remy Martin. Somewhere in between laughing and crying, I can only exclaim over and over again, 'I'm so happy to see you, I can't believe it! Amazing! Thank you so much.' I decide there and then that 26 May will now be known as Saint Mikael's Day. It seems even more appropriate to dedicate a day to him when I discover that amongst Mikael's many achievements, he was actually the first Russian to go round the world by helicopter and to reach the north pole.

The landowner has also come over and kindly offers me a place to sleep for the night. I politely protest until he also says 'hot shower' and I give in. We store the kayak in a shed and drive to his home, 30 minutes away. There I meet his young daughter Anna, a budding gymnast, and we bond over Eurovision before devouring a hearty meal of spaghetti. As I snuggle into bed, pulling the fish-print duvet cover around me, I can't quite believe my luck. One thought goes over and over in my head as I drift off to sleep: a frickin' HELICOPTER.

The next day, I battle against strong winds all day and vow never to complain about flat water feeling monotonous ever again. Progress is slow and painful. I stop early when I see there are limited options for landing as I do not want a repeat of last night's panic. My left hand is also slightly swollen and my body in general is feeling worse for wear. A couple of weeks before the start of the trip, I'd actually torn a ligament in my thumb by landing directly on to it and snapping it backwards during a training session at London Fight Factory. It had just about healed but the scar tissue meant it still felt tight and it was clearly aggravated by me gripping the paddle harder than usual in the wind. Nonetheless, I'd anticipated the first few days would be rough and physical discomfort was to be expected. It'll be a few more days before my body will have adapted to this new regime, and I remind myself to be patient. Whilst setting up my tent, I see empty beer cans from a previous lodger and I feel both anxious at the thought of spending the night in the vicinity of drunken bandits (because I am of course assuming the worst – it would never be family camping!) and cross at the litter.

Soon after pitching my tent, an official looking speed-boat comes over containing two men in uniform. Once again, I assume I'm about to get in trouble. I apologise for not speaking Russian very well and hand over my letter. All is OK; they aren't there to tell me off, they are actually checking if I want some food.

I see them twice more that night and each time they give me a friendly wave as they pass. I laugh a little at how nervous I was to camp here but soon settle in for the night. Eating a dinner of instant noodles and baked beans, I manage to calm my imagination.

The next few days are much the same. Although my targeted daily distance for this section is only 30 miles, even that feels laughable in these conditions. The strong wind turns the previously peaceful river into more of a choppy surfing competition - one I really don't enjoy. The social media attention continues to thrive but with limited access to reception, I'm largely unaware that this side of things is also beginning to stir up, too.

The rocky conditions mean that I have a couple of lower mileage days and one day where I'm unable to paddle at all. I sit out a storm on another beach that seems idyllic until I come across a gigantic tower of rubbish, resembling a small landfill tucked away within the otherwise beautiful nearby woodland. I nickname my temporary home Trash Island and, not for the first time, wish that humans all over the planet weren't so destructive. Litter wasn't a new issue, obviously, I'd seen similar sights in the UK but it is especially sobering to often see stray plastic bottles floating by me on this beautiful river, with no humans in sight but still their rubbish never too far away, wherever you are.

I have a look online as I have signal, and I am infuriated to see that my enforced weather stop has led to some people online telling me that I am not paddling hard enough to reach the Caspian Sea within my 3 month deadline. Less than a week in, and armchair adventurers everywhere suddenly seem to be experts on how far I should be paddling, what I should be eating and where I should be camping. Some are strongly warning me about the dangers of solo camping and others suggesting that Russians are without exception totally angelic and hospitable, so I will be warmly welcomed absolutely everywhere. I suspect, like most places, the reality is that most people really are very kind but it's sensible to be cautious all the same.

My new-found celebrity status, whilst bringing some incredible people into my life, comes with some real challenges, too. I find it difficult to have my every move suddenly scrutinised in this way. Hundreds of messages pour in every day and although the majority of them are full of positivity and offers of help, a few of them are just . . . well, a bit intense and on the weird side. The messages that fall into the 'creepy and unsettling' category cover a broad spectrum, and range from passionate marriage proposals to hostile accusations of being a spy. I learn very quickly that it's a very bad idea to open image files. It's all a bit much and I decide that it's best for me to just focus on the challenge ahead, blocking out as much of the white noise as I can. I recruit some further help back home in dealing with the volume of messages, giving my mum access to the Facebook page and, after warning her to ignore the lunatics, I ask her to highlight any messages from people that mention places where I might be able to grab a shower or a bed for the night along the river.

It is one such message from a kind stranger that fortuitously leads me to the Damirov family. Anna lives in Germany but her family live along the banks of the Volga. She reaches out to tell me they would love to help and so it happens that when I come to the first of the nine dams that I need to portage on my journey, I have a whole team ready and waiting for me. Through the power of social media, people have been following my tracker and coordinating to meet me at the dams so they can provide assistance. Anna's younger brother, Misha, her father, Alexander, and Natasha, her mother, are joined by a few more people, all of whom have been loyally following my journey and are also keen to help. I arrive to a small crowd cheering enthusiastically.

Having previously exited my kayak hundreds of times without incident, I now totally misjudge the water depth and tumble clumsily out of my kayak whilst trying to exit onto the bank. Typically, the one time I have an audience I look like a right muppet. I am completely drenched and covered in mud from the slippery scramble on to land – any illusions I may have had of being an intrepid adventurer quickly vanish. What can you do but laugh? I'm still giggling to myself at the surreal nature of the whole situation as I'm introduced to everyone, whilst doing my best to look like the professional kayaker they all think I am. Misha is also laughing but politely trying to hide it.

Portaging a fully loaded kayak over a dam is usually a

sweaty, laborious affair, and not something that I was looking forward to. However, I don't have to lift a finger at this one. Natasha quickly orders Misha into action and everyone – including the security guards at the dam – make light work of carrying my bags, paddles and kayak up and over the dam. I try to help but am quickly ushered away. This would have taken me ages by myself and I certainly wouldn't have been able to do it in a single trip. However, thanks to my many helpers, within a few minutes, Ariel and all of my gear is on the other side of the river and ready to continue.

The Damirov family wave me on my way and tell me to look out for their house further down the river – they have planted a flag outside so I can't miss it. By now, I have lost count of the amount of times Russian hospitality and the kindness of strangers has left me speechless.

Arriving a couple of hours later at the Damirov home, I am once again treated like royalty. I am introduced to two more members of the clan – a grandmother, who speaks no English but beams warmth at me through her wise, knowing eyes – and family friend Adalat, a keen kayaker himself who enthusiastically bridges the language gap using Google Translate on my iPad. Within minutes, I am made to feel like one of the family. With them, I experience my first Russian sauna – otherwise known as a *banya*. I'd heard *banyas* mentioned and knew vaguely that sticks are involved but otherwise had no idea what to expect. It is a rather surreal experience when I find myself totally naked with Natasha, who I've only known for a couple of hours, in the Damirov family sauna in their garden as she gently tickles me with some soft reeds – all the way down the back of my body as I lie face down and then the same is repeated as I turn over and awkwardly giggle, looking up at the ceiling.

I rest for two days with my newly adopted family. Meanwhile, my clothes are washed and I am taken sightseeing around the small town of Selizharovo– which includes the slightly surreal private tour of the local museum, with the local press in attendance, and then the more peaceful tour of Alexander's beehive. I think I could rival Winnie the Pooh with my love of honey, and I've been enjoying fresh honey from these bees since arriving – in porridge, in coffee or often just by the spoonful.

Well-fed and well rested, it is time for me to get back on the river. Alexander has packed a tub of honey to take with me and Adalat has made me a packed lunch, while constantly emphasising the need for me to eat more. 'Energy,' he says, pointing to the tupperware and doing a mock strong arm flex. 'Energy!'

I hug them all goodbye and as I gradually paddle into the distance, I look back to see them all still waving from the shore

Whilst I've been recharging with my adopted Russian family, I've continued to attract attention on social media: hundreds of messages continue to pour in and a dedicated group on VK.com has formed. Even with help back home, I can't keep up with the sheer volume. I tried to translate as many messages on VK.com as I could whilst I had the use of WIFI at the Damirov home, but there was only so much time I could spend doing that.

I try to ignore the growing unease I feel – the number of sinister messages is steadily increasing and the sheer scale of the publicity makes me much more vulnerable than I'd like. Even delaying the public feed from my satellite tracker and strategically switching it off when approaching the end of the day and scouting for a place to sleep, I'm uncomfortably aware that thousands of people are now literally watching my every move. Head down, eyes on the finish line, I tell myself. I've got a long way to go yet.

The next couple of days drift by, my body now aches less, and it seems I have at last settled into a rhythm. Long, tiring days lead to peaceful evenings at idyllic campsites. There are few things more satisfying than collapsing into a tent after a day of physical effort. At times, it feels like I have this river all to myself. I remind myself to savour it all because I know that soon I am heading into more populated areas. As I steadily edge forwards, I feel my confidence growing and more and more – this river feels like home.

Mikael, the helicopter pilot, has a daughter my age and continues to check in on me – he sources a satellite phone for me to use for my trip and firmly reminds me that if there is anything I need, I am to let him know so he can fly to me. Mikael becomes a friend and guardian angel all in one and the spectacle of him appearing from the sky never gets old. A frickin' helicopter.

One evening, he casually drops in just to bring me some more chocolates. Unfortunately, he also brings a friend, Alex, with him. In stark contrast to Mikael's warm, laid back and good humoured personality, Alex is much more stern and seems to be completely without a sense of humour. He wastes no time in proudly showing me his official Bear Grylls knife and immediately begins to run through what he deems to be essential wilderness skills with me. Both of them seem deeply concerned at my habitual lack of fire building - not appreciating that this was a decision I often made because I was trying to keep a low profile whilst wild camping. It also doesn't seem to matter to them that I have a camping stove, warm sleeping bag and down jacket with me – and that it's summer – they insist I should be building a fire every night, that it is mandatory for both keeping warm and for cooking food.

I get a crash course in selecting the right bark and how best to build a fire. The 'lesson' gets filmed and, not for the first time, I am made out to be a clueless damsel in distress. Naturally, Alex, the knight in shining armour swooping in to save the day. No doubt it's mostly well intentioned, but it's also incredibly patronising. I do my best to focus on the good intentions and not on the fact that Alex's rather large ego has gatecrashed an otherwise lovely evening.

A few days later, I run into a father and son kayaking on the river. Being in an inflatable tandem kayak they are slightly slower than me but we seem to hopscotch around each other all day – them overtaking me when I stop for a break, me catching up and overtaking them later, only for the process to be repeated a couple more times. They have heard about the journey I'm on and were hoping to bump into me – the father, Dimitry, has brought me a present of fridge magnets from the local town. It's a touching gesture and I'm still amazed that so many people seem to have been captured by this journey. At every meeting, we have a lovely chat and, as the day nears its end, we are paddling side by side and both agree it will soon be time to stop for the day. We decide to camp together that night – it's been a few days since I've had much conversation with anyone and I'm excited to have some company. This simple decision will prove to be one of the luckiest twists of fate of the whole trip.

We eat dinner by the fire, warming up and refuelling after a tough but rewarding day on the water. At 9.30, we decide it's time for sleep as we're planning to get up early the next morning to tick off a few more miles. As I make my way back to my tent, I hear someone shouting my name from the opposite bank.

'Laura, Laura Kennington. LAURA!!! LAURA KENNINGTON! You CRAZY!'

The shouting continues along these lines, with the general gist being that they had followed my tracker map to find me. However, I'd switched off the tracker earlier that afternoon and had decided to camp on the opposite side of the river bank—meaning this excitable assembly were unable to reach us. Dmitry flicked his finger at his throat – a gesture referring to alcohol – and shook his head. They were definitely drunk and he made it clear that not all of what they were saying was pleasant.

I call Mum in disbelief at the scale of publicity and thankful for the near miss we'd had. I don't want to worry her, but I feel like this situation is tipping towards being out of control. I speak to Mikael, too, who tells me to keep him posted, promising to fly to the campsite if needed. I reassure him that won't be necessary, and after a couple of hours of sitting by the fire with Dmitry, my nerves calm.

Dmitry is keen to impress upon me just how public this trip had become – the closer I get to the more populated areas, he warns, the more likely this type of group visit is going to be. It's baffling to me that I am now dealing with the side effects of being a celebrity. The implications for my safety are huge. My mind starts to race with what this means for the nature of my journey, but I decide that, whatever the situation, it's not wise to begin brainstorming about it when I am so very tired. Ultimately, it was a bit weird, and the group had temporarily disrupted things, but it was largely harmless and it had all ended well enough.

At 11pm I am tucked up in my sleeping bag and drifting off to sleep. That is until it becomes apparent that the group from earlier are now assembled outside of my tent and demanding an audience with me. They had driven for a further three hours to arrive on the other side of the river and at our campsite, cans of beer in hand. As I emerge from my tent, they are all taking my picture. One of them justifies this intrusion with the explanation that they had written to me on Facebook, but I hadn't replied, and they wished to provide dinner and company tonight—right this very instant, in fact!

However arguably innocent their original intentions, I'm not alone in finding the situation disorienting. Dmitry does his best with me to calm down the excitable rabble, whilst also standing his ground and trying not to let it show how unsettled we both feel. He makes it clear that this situation needs to be handled carefully. Truthfully, we are outnumbered and we both feel very uncomfortable. Amidst all the chaos, I also feel a growing sense of guilt for having unwillingly inflicted this absurdity on a father and his son, Vanya, who – like me – were only hoping to go for a simple paddling trip, perhaps reconnecting to a more peaceful life for a while.

The group remain oblivious to our growing unease and continue to dismiss our objections as totally irrelevant. The ridiculous situation continues; it seems personal space is apparently an alien concept to most of them as they lean in uncomfortably close to me. One man rants about the historical significance of the local area; another quizzes me about the book I would write about my trip and demands to know about my love life; another sets about trying to organise a press conference with me in the next town. All the while, they continue to pose next to me for photographs or to hand over gifts, as if the latter somehow makes their late night intrusion perfectly reasonable. A very long 45 minutes later, that felt like at least two hours, I manage to get the group to reluctantly leave by promising them that I will visit them the next night, in the next town.

When the last of the group have gone, the three of us heave a heavy sigh of relief. Dmitry apologises that he couldn't do more to deter them and, whilst reassuring him that he has nothing to apologise for, I apologise to him for having attracted this situation in the first place.

Collapsing back into my tent, I feel simultaneously furious with the whole situation and completely helpless. I'm shaking with rage and shaking with fear: it is impossible to know the ratio between the two. One thought keeps going over and over in my mind – 'What if I'd have been camped by myself tonight?' I always camped by myself – it was pure chance that I had company tonight. Without Dmitry there to translate and calm things down, it nauseates me to think how the already delicate situation could have been very different and, more importantly, how perhaps I wouldn't be so lucky next time.

I don't sleep at all. Every crackle of a nearby twig, every gust of wind sets my heart racing. Adrenaline surges around my body. Had they come back? What would we do now?

Mikael arrives the next morning and envelopes me in a huge bear hug. He had been worried since our late night chat and says he is relieved to see me – the feeling was totally mutual. Unfortunately, he has brought Alex with him who, after telling me the disruption was entirely my fault and that I should have been more careful in choosing a campsite, decides to capitalise on his visit by filming an interview with me. Mikael plays the role of interviewer as his English is stronger than Alex's and, importantly for any audience, his personality is also much more charming. I do my best to smile my way through it, praising the warm hospitality that I'd received so far, all the while wanting nothing more than for Alex to turn off the camera and for the ground to swallow me up so I might at least have some space to process things.

It's Mikael's birthday and, in celebration, he's brought some lamb kebabs – marinated in his own special recipe – and some wine. I'd actually been vegetarian since I was eight but had purposely reintroduced meat into my diet on a temporary basis a couple of months ago in preparation for this trip. Lots of people seem to think a vegetarian/vegan diet is worryingly protein deficient and therefore not a good match for endurance challenges, and whilst I don't agree with that – I actually both feel and perform better on a plant based diet – my main concern was limiting my food options (and therefore calories in general!) in remote places and I didn't want to be in the position of possibly offending people by rudely turning down food offered through local hospitality. It wasn't ideal but I think it proved to be a good decision throughout my time in Russia, as nearly every meal I was offered was heavily based around either meat or fish.

After a few minutes of laughing over the fire with Mikael, I begin to feel the grey cloud of the previous night lifting. Intuitively sensing that even a riverside birthday party wasn't quite enough to lift my mood completely, Mikael takes me for a private flight in his helicopter. Flying high above the river I've grown to love so much, I feel humbled. I look down on the river as it snakes its way into the distance as far as I could see and the challenge again feels completely overwhelming – the physical distance of this mighty river now being the least of my concerns given the overwhelming levels of public attention.

Back on land, I formulate a plan. Dmitry and I decide that he and Vanya will paddle up ahead acting as a decoy for the local press/over enthusiastic late night visitors who would be looking out for my arrival. Meanwhile, I'd spoken to the Damirov family who were going to come and pick me up.

Hilariously, our decoy was so successful that to this day there is an eight minute film called 'Looking for Laura' on YouTube that features a news crew searching for me in earnest and getting initially very excited to see Dmitry, who they know I've been travelling with, but then very confused that I'm not with him. 007 eat your heart out.

What I need is space to have a thorough look at the situation. It's no good burying my head in the sand any longer. It's clear that the novelty of my challenge isn't wearing off and, if anything, the publicity is only growing stronger. Settling once more into the spare room of the Damirov home, I arrange a Skype call with dear friend and fellow adventurer Dave Cornthwaite to consider how best to handle the situation.

The first time I'd met Dave he was attempting to break the world record for the longest ever game of football with another friend of mine. I'd turned up to help out as an official witness. They were 30 hours into the game by the time I arrived, so in an attempt to boost morale, I came dressed in a penguin onesie, with pom poms, figuring what they all actually needed was a penguin cheerleader. A solid friendship had built from that silly meeting and Dave has been a constant beacon of support and adventure advice ever since.

Later that night, I also manage to Skype another adventurer bestie, Anna McNuff, who is in the middle of running solo across New Zealand. The first time I'd met Anna I'd been doing an all day rowathon in an exhibition centre and she had turned up with a gigantic hug and some homemade beetroot brownies in support. Both of us being rather excitable characters, we'd also been firm friends ever since. In the midst of all the usual adventure chat (mileages, blisters, fatigue, food), Anna provides some welcome distraction by confessing to me she has a huge crush on a boy called Jamie back home – which, naturally, then takes priority for the rest of our conversation.

As my head swirls with all the chaos and turmoil, it's a huge comfort to have a chat with these precious friends of mine. It grounds me at a time when I feel like everything else is spinning out of control.

After brainstorming with Dave, I decide that I will put out a very carefully worded public statement, explaining what had happened the night before, and that I would be taking some time off the river to assess my options and consider some very real safety concerns that had come about as a result of the trip becoming so hugely popular. I'd confessed to Dave that I just didn't feel safe continuing by myself – I felt too vulnerable with this much attention, now my celebrity status seemed to be acting as a potential beacon for any sinister characters.

Essentially, I'm not ready quit, but it no longer feels like a reasonable risk – the booming publicity has totally changed the odds. I really, really don't want to offend the majority of Russian people, who had been so very kind, so I end the blog with:

"I want to express sincere and heartfelt thanks for all the kindness and generosity I have experienced so far– I'm happy to say that this has been the majority of my experience and has surpassed all expectations. Russia is a beautiful country and one I have already such fond memories of. I am considering my options to continue; how best to do it safely and how to minimise any future hindrances.

I would be really keen to hear from fellow kayakers who

might be able to perhaps join me for a few days or for a particular section and by doing so might also be able to provide a bit more security and assistance in continuing the simple journey I set out to do.

I greatly appreciate all the thoughtful and warm support I have received so far and I'm very much looking forward to getting back on the water as soon as possible!"

Reaching out to other kayakers had been Dave's suggestion. We thought that having some fellow paddlers with me might buffer some of the risk and also involve the communities in a more controlled way.

Purposely, I left out any sensational details that might stir things up, but even so the blog only seems to make things worse, turning a delicate situation into an even more volatile one. Although many people reacted warmly and wished me well, there's outrage from others, with many commenting that I was insulting Russians everywhere by implying there would be any danger at all. Furthermore, by suggesting anything even remotely negative, some state that I am lying just to perpetuate negative stereotypes. No matter how many positive things I said about Russia and the kind people that had characterised much of my journey, it's drowned by a frothing sea of angry controversy.

As with the initial flurry of excitement, I rather hope this will die down also. It was naive of me. But after nine months of working ferociously hard to get here, all I want to do is paddle and I desperately hope that somehow I'll find a solution. The Royal Geographical Society (both in London and in Russia) are consulted, amongst others, and yet more frantic Skype conversations are held – all with the sole aim of trying to work out a way for me to continue.

Amongst other things, I am repeatedly told that any 'public disturbances' would be deemed to be my fault and therefore would garner limited sympathy with the police, even if those disturbances resulted in any harm to me. It was a lose-lose situation: heed caution in the face of various threats and I'm apparently damaging international relations. Alternatively, ignore the danger signs and I'd inevitably be blamed and branded foolish.

I am astounded that so many people who don't know me, or indeed the details of the situation, nevertheless feel so entitled to dispense unsolicited advice, vicious criticism and poorly informed opinions about what I should be doing. I wonder how many of the people (mostly male) who are so quick to dismiss my concerns as nonsense and chastise my actions had ever had to deal with direct threats to their safety. Or indeed how many of them would advise their daughters, sisters, wives/girlfriends, or mothers to carry on and blindly ignore multiple threats of sexual assault. Yes, of course it's undoubtedly a tiny minority of people out there who actually pose a threat, but it's significant to me all the same. It would be ludicrous and completely irresponsible to ignore it, especially considering how vulnerable I am on the river.

So I remain at the Damirov home in secret, hiding away in the spare room trying desperately to fix things. All the while, I'm growing steadily more and more morose as I spend hours staring in exasperation at the screen and the chaos that continues to unfold. I get so many warm and wonderful messages of support but they don't inoculate me against the malicious hostility and sickening, stomach-turning threats that also get directed towards me: each and every harsh word I read against me written by hundreds of complete strangers hurts much more than it should. I know deep down that I shouldn't let it in – the people I both love and respect, including fellow adventurers I'd gotten to know over the years, rally around me from afar and these are the people who matter. Nonetheless, the sheer scale of it is overwhelming.

I decide to take my tracker map, which was getting upwards of 8,000 views each day, offline immediately. The genius behind the map, Ant at ZeroSixZero later told me that my map had broken all previous records for viewings. Nevertheless, 24 hours later a stranger on the internet decides to create an unofficial replacement tracker map. This map has green markers which represent my estimated positions and people are told to update the map if they see me. 'Spotters' take to the water, often travelling up and down the river to try and figure out where I am.

A sense of hopelessness building, I barely leave the spare room of the Damirov family, venturing out only reluctantly for meals. The rest of the time, I make more phone calls and spend hour after hour trawling through the internet, desperate for a sign that things have blown over sufficiently for me to get back on the river. Alex infuriates me when he takes it upon himself to speak on my behalf and issue various statements that I have had nothing to do with full of utter rubbish. Even in the midst of a crisis, he continues to try and cash in on the affiliation – as per usual painting himself out to be a hero.

Like any good mother, Natasha lovingly but firmly kicks me out every so often to get some fresh air. Intermittently, the grandmother also pops her head round and insists I follow her to the kitchen for more food. The latter happens several times a day.

Two weeks pass like this. The Damirov's constantly refuse the notion that I should stay somewhere else and also absolutely insist that I don't return to the river until it is considerably safer. It's their unconditional love and hospitality that lightens the otherwise difficult days. I am still there when the grandmother celebrates her ninetieth birthday and Natasha insists I stop sulking in my room and come to join the celebrations. As much as I initially protest, I know she is right and my ever-declining mental state will not improve by locking myself away in the spare room. There is a small band playing in honour of the occasion and I take my seat with the special few that are assembled. Ten minutes later I am joined by a journalist who – delighted at having solved the mystery of where I have disappeared to – begins to press me about when I will return to the river, notebook in hand.

Inwardly, I explode. I get up without saying a word and flee back to the sanctuary of the spare room. It's childish, rude and feels like a very embarrassing way to behave, but on the verge of screaming, I don't know what else to do. Natasha arrives soon after and reassures me that the journalist has promised to not publicise anything, and she pleads with me to come back out and join the family.

Thankfully, the party continues with the grandmother being largely unaware of the disruption. All the same, I conclude that it is time for me to leave. I make the decision to move into a hotel to have one final assessment of what to do. I am craving peace, privacy and quiet. Adalat generously drives me to Moscow – a trip that takes us all day. I don't think I will ever be able to thank the heroic Damirov family and Adalat enough for all of their help and kindness. Most of all, for being a constant reminder of the goodness in people – at a time when I was seeing some of the worst.

THREE WEEKS of relentless assessment has lead to an

inescapable conclusion: it is time to fly home. There is no way to sufficiently mitigate the risks and I don't feel justified in continuing under such circumstances. I've also grown fed up of the whole circus. There is a fine line between being a badass and dumbass; I wasn't going to be bullied into making a stupid decision for the sake of saving my ego. Persevering through physical fatigue and mental struggles is a battle I consider worth fighting – risking my safety and juggling with security amidst public mayhem is not a fight I want to continue any longer. It's time for me to tap out.

I book a flight back to the UK – six weeks earlier than planned – and decide that I will issue the statement when I'm safely home to avoid any more potential disruptions. I have two days to get everything ready. In those two days, I take Elvira out to lunch to say thank you and Mikael arranges for a car to pick up his satellite phone from the hotel. Alex is told I am leaving at a later date and, like everyone else, is asked to please keep the news quiet, for security reasons.

Boarding the flight back home, I am heartbroken and deflated. But I am also relieved. For six weeks I have had my every move scrutinized and I am exhausted from the constant effort of having to navigate the delicate and volatile situation. Touching down at Heathrow, greeted by an extremely relieved Mum, I burst into happy-exhausted-sad tears. I am safe, I am home and no one here has a clue who I am. Blissful anonymity! I can say with absolute certainty that I've never been so thankful to see British soil.

Before I've even unpacked my expedition gear or finished my first cup of tea, I want to fully close this chapter and I sit down to publish the announcement. Only to realise that Alex has taken it upon himself – again – to release an 'official' statement on my behalf, after another fictitious conversation we haven't had, citing yet more patronising nonsense that I haven't sanctioned. It's not a huge surprise, he was always pleasant enough to my face but then wouldn't waste any time in mocking me from the comfort of his computer screen. I am relieved to already be home and therefore out of reach of any public backlash. At the bottom of my own statement on my website I include the following in a final attempt to shut down Alex's ridiculous ego-fuelled attention-grabbing nonsense:

"It has been brought to our attention that some individuals in Russia misrepresented themselves as part of the official team. Please note that all enquiries go through the team here in the UK only. There is not now, nor has there ever been, any other official representative in Russia."

Not that it mattered much anymore now, but after weeks of enduring his backstabbing and slimy drivel, it was a satisfying moment all the same.

As the news spreads, my email inbox explodes and my phone is ringing constantly with journalists wanting to capitalise on the sensational story. I speak to none of them. I want no part in this – I'd discovered that no matter how much I try to emphasise that the majority of Russians I encountered were extremely kind and generous, that isn't the story they want to write. It wasn't the story that some people were willing to hear directly from me either – it was much easier to mock and berate me from the comfort of their armchairs instead.

"'I'm sorry men didn't f*** her": British woman, 28, abandons solo charity kayak in Russia after receiving "very sinister" threats' is the classy headline that British tabloid newspaper *The Daily Mail* leads with, the rest of the article following a predictably sensational and distasteful tone. I ignore common sense and some sage advice and make the mistake of reading the comments section of this very article. History repeats itself as I trawl through pages and pages of strangers spewing out bile and venom about me, for reasons I can't understand.

A large amount of them seemed enraged that I was using such a huge expedition to raise money for charity, bitterly arguing that I could have used the trip budget as a donation instead. Inwardly, my blood boils at the sheer audacity of so many strangers who think they have the right to have a say in my life. The facts – in which no one seemed in the least bit interested – are that I'd self-funded this challenge through months of working three simultaneous jobs as it was something I wanted to do for personal reasons anyway. I'd merely figured that if I could raise money for a good cause at the same time, having already covered the actual expedition costs myself, then that made total sense. Every single penny raised through my fundraising had gone directly to the charity. I didn't see anyone berating marathon runners for their efforts to raise funds and awareness for good causes through physical endeavour. What exactly was so terrible about that? What exactly about that had made people delight in my failure so much?

Despite my best efforts to stay positive, this failure and the controversial negativity that surrounds it seeps into my soul like a virus and, unable to shake it off, I spiral into depression. As the initial relief of coming home fades, the legacy of the hugely public failure hangs over me like a dark and inescapable shadow. The story takes on a life of its own and eventually I conclude that all I can do is starve it of oxygen, wait for it to die down and, in the long term, outlast it.

For weeks, all I want to do is hide under the duvet, with my phone switched off. It's all I can do to force myself out long enough to go training for a couple of hours every week at London Fight Factory and, had it not been for these sessions, I would have largely been a total recluse. My first foray into endurance adventure has been a complete disaster. It is, to say the least, a hugely humbling experience.

3 GET BACK UP

'Life shrinks or expands in proportion to one's courage'
– Anais Nin

Perhaps my only real credential in taking on endurance challenges is the same quality that I hope will now see me through this – stubbornness. 'Girl attempts to kayak Russian river – it all goes wrong and, never quite recovering from the awkward embarrassment of it all, she is never heard from again' – I refused for this to be my story. I decide that the best way to silence the criticism, both coming from other people and from inside my own head, is to take action. I am desperate for people to have something else to talk about and even more desperate to have something else to think about, so I decide to call an end to my sulking and instead channel my frustration into something more productive. Angrily fighting against things I couldn't change wasn't going to change the situation anytime soon, but it is changing me – and not for the better.

I didn't want to be bitter and twisted about Russia any more. It is time to let it go and follow some good old-fashioned advice from a childhood nursery rhyme:

For every ailment under the sun
There is a remedy, or there is none;
If there be one, try to find it;
If there be none, never mind it.
Mother Goose – wise old bird!

An invite to my uncle's wedding in Ireland is all the opportunity I need. Months before, I'd seen a TV program whilst at a friend's house about the Wild Atlantic Way – the world's longest coastal route, which spans 1,600 miles across the west coast of Ireland. I purposely don't own a TV, so the chances of me seeing this program were slight, but I made a mental note of it at the time, putting the route on the never-ending list of potential adventures. 'Someday,' I thought. Well, it seemed that someday had arrived. I decided I was going to cycle across Ireland en route to my uncle's wedding. I'd start in Belfast and make my way south along the coast until reaching the end of the route in Cork. My uncle's wedding would actually be in Westport, situated more towards the middle of the route but mum had kindly agreed to to fly into Cork and pick me up in a rental car, bringing some clean clothes for me to wear to the wedding in her suitcase.

In stark contrast for the nine months of meticulous planning that went into the Caspian Challenge, I have just two weeks to pull together what I'd, perhaps unimaginatively, named the 'Wild Atlantic Ride'. Although I don't have visa issues to contend with this time, if I leave any later I run the risk of missing my uncle's wedding, the timing already being rather tight! I still have the same road bike, which is not especially designed for touring, so I decide to just pack as light as possible and hope Dory survives. I don't have much time to do any training either.

A lot of the basic kit I needed, (like a tent and camping stove, etc) carried over from Russia and the rest of the necessary items I manage to piece together and borrow where necessary, also making sure to watch some YouTube clips on how to fix a puncture. A rough route plan gives me a timetable of four weeks. I decide to ignore the fact that I haven't been on my bike for months and instead focus on the success of my early cycling endeavours – success being a relative term, by which I mean that although it had been very painful (arguably much more painful than it needed to be because I hadn't prepared properly and I didn't have a clue what I was doing), I'd still successfully arrived to where I'd needed to go both times. That was all that mattered. I tell myself that my legs will adapt in time. In truth, there are hundreds of reasons why I'm not ready to do this trip, but I can't stomach the failure of Russia any longer. I plan, quite literally, to escape it. A hastily scrambled plan is now formed and I am on an overnight ferry to Belfast, stomach gurgling full of nerves again, getting ready for another adventure. In some ways, the start of the Wild Atlantic Ride is even harder than Russia – I have demons to face now, their harsh words ringing in my head – compounded by the familiar nerves and words of self-doubt that I know so well. What if I fail this one, too? I tell myself repeatedly that I will just do my best and I hope that will be enough.

To save money, I opt against getting a cabin for the overnight ferry crossing. Instead, I pull my buff over my eyes and turn up the music (opting for the soothing piano music of Ludovico Einaudi) in my headphones whilst attempting to sleep, awkwardly curled up on a chair in the onboard ferry cinema. Meanwhile, nearby slot machines whirr and an increasingly rowdy crowd sing and shout their way through the evening. Thankfully, my seasickness pills make me drowsy so I still get a solid four hours of sleep despite the surrounding chaos.

At 5am, even the hardiest of beer drinkers are peacefully snoring away and I sneak out on deck to see the sunrise. The waters are glassy calm and I shiver in the crisp morning air as I watch the sky slowly turn from black, to pink and then to orange. An uninterrupted horizon and a sunrise is a flawless combination – no matter where I am in the world and how I feel, it's something that can always set my mind at ease. It's a simple but powerful reminder of the planet's magic.

After an initially sunny welcome, the first day is full of unrelenting rain and wind. By the time I finish for the day, 80 miles later, I am covered in grit and dripping wet. I have temporary tan lines created by dirt but I can't stop grinning and I feel happier than I have in weeks. I was back on solid ground – with a goal to focus on and a finish line to reach.

I end day two feeling considerably less triumphant – my legs are ready to disown me. Apparently, the West Coast of Ireland is extremely hilly – a fact that is seemingly well known but still somehow escaped me completely in my all too brief planning phase. Optimistically ignorant of the terrain that awaited, it never once occurred to me to check the elevation of the route when planning my daily targets.

All of day two is spent pushing my loaded bike up the never-ending hills. Suddenly, my estimated mileage of 70 miles for the day seems completely unrealistic. I have covered half of the distance in double the time I'd planned. Thinking I might be able to cut across the coast and miss out some of the hills, I zoom down a steep hill full of switchbacks. On reaching the beach at the bottom, I see that it's actually a dead end. The thought of making it back up the monumental hill is too much – my legs have turned to jelly and I'm knackered. I decide I will camp there for the night – even if it is only 3pm.

Leaving Dory resting on the nearby grass verge, I walk along the beach to scope it out. At one end, a man is already camped with a huge eight-man tent. I tentatively ask him if it's private property or if it's OK for me to camp there too. He happily introduces himself and tells me that he is no more official than I am, but people camp here every year. Chris is here with his family and cheerily informs me that I'm welcome to camp wherever I like. It's a small thing, being able to have a conversation like this, but after the language barriers of Russia it's one I feel immensely thankful for. This will be my first time wild camping since Russia and my mind races – the illogical part of my brain waging a war against the calmer, more rational side. I run through several worst case (read: completely ridiculous) scenarios:

What if the (really lovely) man called Chris I just spoke to is actually a serial killer, who now knows that I'm planning to camp on the beach, too? Is that even his real name? Have I just made myself a really easy target?

It's a ridiculous train of thought, with no basis at all on Chris's actual character. He offered me a cup of tea – with biscuits – and passed on some knowledge on the local area, too. Hardly the sort of behaviour that one would classify as cause for alarm. I remind myself of how statistically unlikely it is to bump into serial killers – and even more unlikely that one would just happen to pitch up on the largely deserted beach waiting for a lone female to pray on. I also reason that even if he is a serial killer (which, logically, I'm 99.9 per cent sure he isn't), I'm too tired to get back up that hill anyway, so there's nothing to be done.

In times of irrational worry (and, let's face it, most worries are irrational) I always try to consider the law of averages for that particular situation. It's a good reality check and reminds me that, usually, whatever I'm working myself into a frenzy over is extremely unlikely to ever occur. Ultimately, my assessment usually follows a formula like this:

What are you worried about?

How likely is that to happen?

What, if anything, can you do to lessen that risk?

Logic and fear don't often coexist peacefully, the latter is usually fuelled by my imagination running wild – no doubt resulting from my guilty pleasure of watching too many horror films with my friend Siobhan. We must have watched hundreds over the years, covering every possible terrifying (and highly unlikely) combination of events. And so I always find running through a sensible checklist very calming and reassuring. I try to adopt a healthy scepticism of the negative headlines that paint a misleading and sinister view of this world and let the law of averages do most of my worrying for me instead. So often what we worry about doesn't happen. Worse still, we're so worried that it will happen, that sometimes we don't even try. I think deep down we all know we shouldn't worry about things we can't do anything about. We say things like, 'Cross that bridge when you come to it' and 'No use crying over spilt milk', but I don't know how often we really listen to the common sense contained within. I constantly try to remind myself to focus on the mile I am riding, and not stress about the miles ahead of me and what they might contain. Focusing on the next step – and only that – is good advice for life in general, but I find it essential for endurance challenges.

Setting up my little tent on a grassy mound with an incredible view of the immense cliff that overlooks the sea, the last rays of light dancing across the rippling water, I immediately make peace with the fact that I'd only covered half of my targeted distance. I wouldn't want to miss this view for the world. To this day, it remains one of the most beautiful places I've ever wild camped. I have a brief friendly chat with an elderly husband and wife who are leisurely walking along the beach as I begin to pitch my tent. This small conversation also helps to settle any lingering nerves about wild camping again.

Getting ready to cook my standard dinner of noodle surprise (surprise, it's noodles again!), I realise my water bladder has leaked – leaving me with roughly 50ml of water. Not enough to cook with and, more importantly, not enough to keep me hydrated until the next day. I poke my head out of the tent to see a campervan parked up nearby with a family milling around it. I decide to go over and ask if they have any water they could spare.

Before I've even had a chance to ask about the water, Lyndsey and David have placed a burger into one of my hands and a small tumbler of red wine into the other. I am introduced to their two young boys, Harris and Lewis – named after the Scottish isles – and the next couple of hours are spent laughing. I've hardly drank for months, so the wine goes straight to my head. I know I'm going to suffer for it in the morning, but I'm having too much fun to care. It feels like I've known this family for years, not hours. Adventure links people together this way – bonded by similar natures, a common appreciation of the simple things. It's only after a couple of hours that I mention I'd actually only popped over to see if they had any water – this sets us all off laughing again. By anyone's standards, going to get some water and returning with a belly full of burgers and wine is a pretty great deal. Before I retreat back into my tent for the night, they kindly also hand over some insect repellent when I confess iId forgotten to pack mine.

Heading back to my tent, I am greeted by the elderly woman from earlier.

'I've had a chat with my husband and you'd be very welcome to stay with us tonight,' she says warmly 'It's not much but you'd be very welcome.'

I politely decline and reassure her that I've got everything I need, and promise her I will be warm enough. Before she leaves, she gives me her telephone number – just in case.

Snuggling down into my sleeping bag, I can't help but marvel at the small moments of magic that adventures bring. I couldn't have asked for a better reintroduction to wild camping. I take it as a good omen and that I mustn't let the bad experiences in Russia stay with me now. I know that as scary as it's been to pick myself up and venture out again, it was the best possible decision. It feels right to be reclaiming the things I love so much and to not let my surreal experience with a minority taint my world view.

The next morning, David cheerfully brings over some breakfast to my tent. Minutes later, Chris has also appeared with one of his daughters to offer me a morning cup of tea – only to realise that David has beaten him to it! I briefly consider that maybe I could just spend the next four weeks on the world's friendliest beach. As a compromise, David offers me a lift back up the hill and I gratefully accept. I have a rule about not 'cheating' and skipping sections of the route, but I reason that doubling back doesn't count. As the campervan struggles up what feels like a near vertical ascent, any lingering feelings of guilt are replaced by relief – I'm very happy to be tackling this in a car and not by bike, no regrets at all.

This first night sets the tone for the rest of the journey. Although the days are filled with gruelling, punishing hills, I am constantly greeted by kindness and the warmth of the friendly locals never fails. In between camping, I sometimes stay with people I've connected to through a network designed for cycle tourers called Warm Showers.

Within four days, I have to apply KT tape to an increasingly angry Achilles heel – my right foot swells up to the point where I'm unable to fit it into my cleated cycling shoes. I end up cycling in my KEEN sandals instead, which leaves me with rather unique tiger-stripe tan lines on my feet. My legs scream at me all day and often burn each night, although I sleep heavily, helped by the satisfying exhaustion of a day spent battling against the urge to give up.

One day, I inadvertently adopt a stray dog for a few hours in the mountains. Growing slightly concerned that I might accidentally be stealing someone else's adorable dog, I feel relieved when he eventually turns around and heads off, but thankful for his affection and company for the brief time we had.

There are, however, days when it's a herculean task to extract myself out of my oh-so-cosy sleeping bag and face the rain, or days when I find myself alone and hurting – flying down steep descents, only to crawl back up moments later. The Irish terrain is relentless. I'm a week into the trip when – after a few hours of only sheep for company and with legs like jelly – I feel close to tears for the first time. An ultimately harmless but briefly terrifying encounter with three angry dogs as I pass a farmhouse makes me want to cry even more. The problem with emotions is they are so utterly irrational. Mine begin to spiral rapidly, fuelled by tiredness as I climb yet further into the secluded mountains – I want to be enjoying the stunning scenery but my thoughts keep drifting to how easy it would be for my body to never be found in a place like this. It's only 1pm and there's plenty of daylight left to get me back to civilisation, but I still think about how this is the perfect setting for one of those trashy horror films. Note to self: perhaps watch fewer horror films.

On a good day, I relish the solitude and peace of places like this, but this isn't a good day. I distract myself by taking photos and filming, but in truth I am in no mood to be here. At 3pm I am finally coming down out of the hills and heading back to civilisation when it starts to rain – hard. Within minutes I am shivering as I zoom downhill. When I stop to get waterproofs on, I am immediately surrounded by midges. My initial joy at reaching the next town is quickly curbed by another angry dog chasing me, while the owner does nothing to stop him. I take it personally and I feel like screaming back to the dog: 'Oh, stop it – I'm having a rough day here and I'm actually a GOOD PERSON; if you'd JUST get to KNOW ME then YOU'D STOP BARKING.' But instead I lash out with an angry 'HEY!' that seems to do the trick and I keep pedalling. I love dogs. Few things make me happier than meeting new canine friends, especially on an adventure when their furry cuddles can feel extra comforting, and I often feel irrationally betrayed when they turn out to be less than friendly.

I've decided to treat myself to an official campsite with shower facilities, that costs a whopping eight Euros, and I nearly burst into tears with relief when I arrive. Halfway through my hard-earned warm shower, however, there is a power cut and the water turns icy cold. I turn to the second morale boosting strategy of food, glorious food. I devour some pasta in my tent as a starter and then order a large salad at the nearby restaurant for seconds, this being the only thing they can make in a power cut. It works in my favour though – because I usually have to focus on high calorie meals, the salad wouldn't have been my first choice, but it does inject some much needed nutrition and greenery into my diet. Admittedly, though, the nutrition of the apple pie and ice cream I have for desert feels even more amazing. Ice cream fixes everything. I feel a sense of relief and that quiet satisfaction of being totally exhausted but proud for pushing through. I check in to dozens of well wishes on social media and – between this and the ice cream – I feel the worst of the day fade away.

Through every gruelling ascent and through so many tough moments, I am spurred on by the will to put the failure of Russia behind me. I am motivated by the knowledge that every pedal stroke brings me closer to the finish line in Ireland, but perhaps even more importantly that it is one pedal stroke further from the harsh words and controversy of Russia. I picture every armchair critic and trashy newspaper journalist that is willing me to fail and I refuse to give them the satisfaction.

Some days I push myself so hard that I can barely speak at the end of the day. Sometimes I push on through lunch, fuelling on the occasional biscuit as I go, refusing to stop for fear I won't be able to start again because I'm so tired. I cry, I scream – but I refuse to stop moving, even if I have to move slowly. Every day, without fail, the scenery of the Irish mountains blows me away. I begin to finally understand what John Muir meant when he spoke of climbing the mountains to get their good tidings. The simple, pure act of physical exertion and immersion in nature is healing. I am growing stronger and more resilient every day, confidence coming from the simple act of not giving up. With every day that passes, the things that people are saying about Russia seem to matter a lot less.

As I am half Irish on my mum's side, this adventure also comes with the notable perk of having various relatives dotted along the route. I'm not entirely sure how I'm related to some of them but that doesn't seem to matter one bit – I am welcomed in to their homes, fed until I am fit to burst, told hilarious and heart-warming stories of my grandparents, given a comfy bed to sleep in and then sent on my way again.

Margaret and Kevin Kennedy go one further, and whilst I mostly spend my day off on the sofa cuddled up with Aisha the dog, Kevin takes Dory into a bike shop where the rear tyre is replaced and everything is cleaned. A couple of days before arriving into Castlebar to stay with Margaret and Kevin, a thick rogue hook in the roadside had pierced through the rear wheel and the cheap replacement I'd bought from the small bike shop at the time wasn't going to last that long, especially considering the extra weight on the back of the bike. That same bike shop had also accidentally pinched the inner tube when they'd replaced my tyre and I'd then done the same a few miles down the road when fitting a new inner tube, so all together I'd had three puncture incidents in 24 hours. Thankfully, I don't have another one for the rest of the trip.

I also stay with my cousin Luke Cassidy in Galway who I haven't seen in well over a decade. We used to spend a lot of time together when we were younger but as the years had gone by, I hadn't seen much of my cousins. I am greeted by a tall, strapping man – about three times taller than the cute, cheeky little lad I remember.

'The last time I saw you, I could pick you up!' I exclaim.

'Well, you could give it a go if you like,' he replies, laughing.

Luke and his housemates are not as shocked as I expected, and if anything more amused to hear about the horrendous climbs I've battled en route to Galway. I'm beginning to think I'm the only person on the planet who didn't already know about the Irish hills. Luke tells me that there is, in fact, many a song written about the fierce terrain. He plays me 'Hills of Donegal' – it will be stuck in my head for days to come.

I am two weeks into my trip when I am leaving Luke's house. It's at this point I notice that, for the first time, I do not have to get off to push my bike up one of the infinite Irish hills! I take a moment to play 'All Star' by Smash Mouth at full volume through my earphones and do a little celebratory dance at the top of a hill – the rain lashing down and my cheap waterproofs rustling. My cycling legs have finally joined the adventure!

The next day, however, my cycling prowess is put into perspective when I am surrounded by dozens of very colour coordinated cyclists on extremely expensive bikes – I've managed to coincide with the official Race Around Ireland. Each solo cyclist (or in some cases each team of cyclists) has their own dedicated support vehicle, and although part of me feels proud for being self-supported, a much bigger part is immediately envious at the lack of weight they have to carry and that they have a large van, with flashing lights, providing insulation against the traffic.

I have intermittent chats with many of them at various traffic lights. A terribly serious German rider spends a couple of minutes boasting about his daily mileages and sleep deprivation before racing off again as soon as the lights go green. At the next set of traffic lights, I am greeted by a considerably more affable Irish cyclist and after we exchange a couple of jokes about the obscene amount of calories we are both consuming, he commends me on carrying my own gear and wishes me well for the rest of the trip. I conclude that as lovely as it would be to have a support crew, I much prefer doing it this way – it seems a shame to race so quickly through such beautiful scenery. Team tortoise all the way.

As I get closer to the finish line in Cork, I reflect on all this journey has required of me and, in return, all that it has given back. It has demanded sweat, tears and claimed a high toll on my weary muscles – so often it seemed to be asking much, much more than I had.

However, it has provided infinitely more than it has taken – it has given me an inner sense of calm, a quiet confidence in knowing I can rise above obstacles and a calm contentment. For the first time in years, I don't have anywhere else I want to be, anything to prove or anything else I think I should be doing with my life. I grew up reading Irish fairy tales and now, as an adult, I'm more convinced than ever that there's magic in Ireland.

As finish line celebrations go, an Irish wedding is hard to beat. I'm reunited with more cousins and I exchange stories of the landscape with my grandparents. My Nanny Mary is in the final stages of battling cancer and, for a while, we were unsure if she'd be able to make it to the wedding. Nothing is more important to Nanny than family, so it's not a huge surprise that she defiantly fought to be here for my uncle's special day, but it's an impressive feat all the same. She's suffered some hair loss due to chemotherapy but, ever glamorous, she styles it out by wrapping a scarf around her head. It's both heartbreaking and inspiring to see her so frail but determined, clearly in pain but battling on.

Both grandparents on my dad's side passed some years ago, also to cancer. Grandad Norman passed first when I was eight years old and, years later, Nanny Rose followed. I remember Nanny Rose remaining strong and family centred to the end, too. If there are ever feats of endurance worth celebrating, I think it's in the ordinary struggles of everyday life. Any endurance challenge I will ever do pales in comparison to battling cancer.

I'm certain I inherited a great deal of stubbornness from my grandmothers and, of course, my own phenomenal superhero of a mum. I think of these warrior women whenever I struggle, and visualise a legacy of strength and resilience running through my DNA.

I arrive home a different woman than when I left. Whatever controversy may still be lingering from Russia bothers me less now. With the help of the Irish mountains, I have made peace with it.

I FINISH the year by paddling the River Thames, from its source back to London, with my friend Pete Kohler, who'd been a key member of my Russian support team. We decided to do it in the run up to Christmas and therefore affectionately named the challenge 'Paddling Home for Christmas' – naturally making sure to wear Christmas jumpers and Santa hats for the week.

My friend Ed Underwood once more valiantly stepped up for another road trip and gave me a lift to the source of the river in Lechlade, his admirable tolerance for my road trip playlists shining through again. This time I'd made a festive edition, naturally, which included several Christmas carols, including my personal favourites from arguably one of the greatest films of all time – *The Muppet Christmas Carol*.

Pete arrived courtesy of our friend Andy Bartlett. Running through Pete's kit list the pub that night, we discover his preparation had been well-intentioned but a bit questionable. In Pete's defence, he'd been very busy at work in the days leading up to this trip, and I had experience of packing for a kayak adventure, so was perhaps at an unfair advantage. He had managed to purchase a special 'hydrophobic' water repellent base layer especially for the journey, but he'd then neglected to factor in food as well as hydration, so would end up eating half of my porridge every morning. Nevertheless, it was great fun to have an adventure buddy with me for a change.

It was the first time I'd unpacked Ariel since Russia and as I get her ready to launch into the water, I feel a tinge of sadness and guilt for all the miles left unexplored with her. What big plans we'd had! As I take my first few paddle strokes, a rush of emotions comes flooding back as I remember just how nervous and incapable I'd felt in Russia. I think about all the hours of happiness that followed; all the moments of fear and everything in between.

It feels appropriate to be exploring the Thames – it's the second longest river in the UK and one I am very fond of. I've spent countless hours either cycling or walking alongside the Thames as I travel around the hustling busyness of London. It's provided the backdrop for brainstorming sessions, meetings with friends, pensive wanderings and most other things in between.

The early section of the Thames is beautifully quiet

and tranquil – even more so in winter, and it largely feels like we have it to ourselves. Although, heartbreakingly, even this section is full of litter – an issue that get worse the closer to London we paddled. Different river, same toxic influence of humans still sadly present. We remove as much as we can on our way, and Pete is inspired to later go on to launch a phenomenal clean up project called The Plastic Tide, using drone technology to help measure, understand and ultimately address plastic pollution across the UK.

Whilst waiting for companies to catch up and implement significant changes, I think we all have a responsibility in this area as plastic is, literally, choking our planet – with eight million pieces of plastic (80 per cent of which comes from land based sources) finding their way into our oceans every single day. The facts on plastic pollution are shocking and we can (and should!) all do something to help – solid shampoo bars and reusable cutlery/water bottles/thermal mugs/shopping bags are all basic things that help. All rivers lead to the sea of course and so the debris I see from my kayak is a constant and sobering reminder of the issue. Wherever I went, there it was.

It wasn't the most obvious time of year to pick for a kayaking adventure, but it was gorgeous and serene, our breath making clouds of vapour in the icy air . Packing up our tents on the third morning, we are greeted by a breathtaking sunrise that colours the world in dazzling pinks and fiery oranges and makes us forget the frost, if only for a few minutes. The bitter temperatures also provides great motivation to keep moving. We stay warm by paddling and also occasionally by pulling over to the irresistible sight of a riverside pub, where we enjoy a hearty pub lunch and defrost by a roaring fire.

On the final day, I begin to recognise various landmarks

and bridges. We keep the VHF radio close to hand so we can communicate with other river users when necessary. The closer we get to London, the more mindful we'll need to be of the fact that our relatively small kayaks could be tricky to see amongst the busy river traffic It's quite the rollercoaster when we find ourselves frantically paddling past iconic sights such as the Houses of Parliament and the London Eye, our kayaks now rising and falling with the large waves caused by both the wind and the wake from the boats speeding by.

Less than 20 minutes away from our finish point, I have to make a speedy sprint back across to the right side of the river, having been pushed more into the middle by strong currents, and I unintentionally end up racing to get out of the way of a Thames Clipper speeding directly at me. It feels terrifying until I've cleared the path, at which point – with adrenaline coursing through my veins – I victoriously raised my paddle into the air and promptly re-characterised the whole experience as excellent fun.

On 23 December, after eight days and 236 miles of paddling, Pete and I end up at the iconic Tower Bridge – smelly, achy and smiling, with rosy wind-burnt faces. Some friends are waiting in a pub nearby, so we pull the kayaks up the slippery steps, strip off our outer waterproof layers to reveal our Christmas jumpers underneath and headover to begin the merry celebrations. I am really looking forward to not eating porridge or instant noodles again for a while.

It has only been seven months since those first tentative paddle strokes in Russia, but so much has changed. I am a different woman to when I'd started. It feels satisfying to be ending the year with Ariel – a celebration of all that we've overcome and a promise of all the future adventure we still have to look forward to.

4   BREAK THE MOULD

The greatest adventure is what lies ahead
Today and tomorrow are yet to be said
The chances, the changes are all yours to make.
The mold of your life is in your hands to break.
— J.R.R. Tolkien

I started 2016 with a blank slate. I'd decided that I'd try to make a career out of adventure. I didn't know if it was possible but I knew it was worth trying. What was the worst that could happen? The answer to this question was simple and obvious but also incredibly liberating. When I assessed the situation honestly I realised that if it didn't work out, I could always just get another mind-numbingly dull job. But shouldn't I at least try to build a better life? Shouldn't I at least try to explore my potential? The time was going to pass anyway, so I figured that I might as well let it pass whilst working towards something I actually enjoyed and that I felt had value. I'd finally rediscovered my spark and I embraced that I was here to do more than save up for a mortgage. Endurance challenges had added purpose to my days and purpose, I'd learnt, was essential for happiness.

I began building up my speaking career – speaking at schools and also working more with the brands that I'd optimistically contacted in 2015. I get asked a lot for advice about building a career in adventure and especially about working with brands. The only advice I can offer is the approach I always try to take – offer value. For me this means offering honest product feedback, proactively suggesting mutually beneficial projects and community events that we can work together on and and also making sure to consistently share footage of their kit in action, doing what it does best. I was, and still am, so grateful to any brand that first said 'yes' to me. My profile has grown over the years so, in many ways, approaching brands has become a bit easier, but I still remember where it all started. Never take support, no matter how seemingly small, for granted. It's a relationship like any other than needs nurturing to thrive.

In return, I only work with brands that support me as well. I'm not motivated by empty promotions, it has to be the right balance. Similarly, I refuse to endorse anything I don't fully believe in – regardless of how much money might be offered. I've turned down well paid proposals from sugary cereal brands, environmentally careless sportswear companies and countless other things that I just have no need for. I think that anyone in a position to reach a large audience (enter the rise of social media marketing!) has a responsibility with what they promote.

2016 saw my first few speaking engagements at various

festivals for KEEN footwear. I flew to Hamburg to officially represent them as an ambassador at the opening night of the Ocean Film Festival in Hamburg. It was my first time speaking outside of the UK and many of the KEEN team I'd never met before were also in attendance. I remember being so nervous on the huge stage for that first talk that I feared the butterflies in my stomach might cause me to levitate.

As my experience built up, my talks improved and my confidence grew. Earning a living as a speaker, just like anything else, takes time and practice – lots of the latter! I delivered countless talks to schools for free until I'd honed my skills and improved enough to warrant charging anything. And it took even longer for talks to become the pillar of income that it is for me now. My background as an actress certainly helped but I still found it more terrifying than you might think to make the transition – being onstage, playing a character and delivering lines from a script that someone else had written felt so much easier compared to the vulnerability of opening up to tell my own story. There was no script and no character to hide behind any more! I love storytelling now – I've found my voice and I know what I want to say – but it really does take time to build and I've had some key supporters in the wings cheering me on. Having people that believe in you and see your potential is invaluable.

As I continued to pursue speaking engagements, the inevitable 'What's next?' question lingered. I knew that I wanted my next adventure to challenge me in a unique way and I liked the idea of kayaking but didn't want to paddle down another river just yet. I considered that it might be fun to circumnavigate an island instead. I began googling various islands, and when I looked at the Channel Islands something sparked. I couldn't help but notice that actually three of the islands were rather close together. The map seemed to be screaming 'TRIATHLON'. I loved the idea of packing three different mini adventures into one. Organised events have never really appealed to me, but making up my own inter-island triathlon filled me with an irrepressible excitement. I had my next challenge.

A standard triathlon consists of a running section, a swimming section and a cycling section. However, having convinced myself for many years that I definitely wasn't a runner, I decided that my triathlon would in fact have a kayaking section instead of a running section. My triathlon, my rules. The plan is to swim around Sark, to kayak around Guernsey and then to cycle around Jersey. First things first, I needed to improve my swimming. The distance around Sark is five miles – the swimming equivalent of a marathon. (Marathon swimming is usually defined by swims of 10km or more,

I was immediately pointed in the direction of Mark Kleanthous – otherwise known as Ironmate Mark. Mark has completed 40 Ironman triathlons and more than 500 triathlons overall. He came well recommended by my friend Sean Conway, who had recently become the first person to swim the length of Britain. If there was anyone who could help me successfully go from relative newbie to marathon swimmer in a few months, it was Mark.

Mark's infinite knowledge is matched only by his boundless positivity and support. At a time when many people were telling me I was being over ambitious and were quick to recount the story of people who'd apparently died attempting to swim around Sark, Mark was immediately in my corner. He designed me a training program to follow, which included weekly pool swimming and road cycling sessions, as well as one session each week dedicated to strength and conditioning in the gym. I also gained support from the lovely ladies behind Tri 'n' Swim Well, a swimming school based in Essex – they not only provided me with my wetsuit but also further helped improve my swimming technique and passed on the game-changing bit of advice to get customised ear plugs made.

Russia taught me to always filter criticism and not just automatically let it in – who is it coming from and is there any authority behind their comments? Why should you pay attention to it? I'd learnt that, unfortunately, people some-times liked to tear down others just to make themselves feel better and gain some sort of mean-spirited gratification, and I'd vowed that these weren't people I would ever let influ-ence my decisions. The people who believed I could do it were those with relevant experience and they were also people I admired – I decided that those were the opinions it made sense to listen to.

AS I LAND IN GUERNSEY, the butterflies in my stomach are doing unprecedented levels of acrobatics. I've come here for a recce ahead of the challenge in June, now just four months away. Open water swimming is a whole new sport to me and my head is reeling with all the logistics: support boat, support kayaker, feeding schedule, tides. The Channel Islands are home to the third largest tidal range (the difference between high tide and low tide) in the world and, while understanding the basics, I'm definitely not confident enough to plan my route by myself – it's too important to risk making a mistake in this area. The direction of the tidal stream is especially relevant to me – I definitely won't win if I try to fight it by swimming against it.

Luckily for me, the Channel Islands has a huge culture of open water swimming and the locals in general are an adventurous bunch. They are also incredibly warm and welcoming. A few months back, I'd been introduced via email to Guernsey resident and open water swimming legend Adrian Sarchet, known to his friends as Ady, and now I found myself welcomed into his home and meeting his wonderful wife Andy (and getting to cuddle their two dogs, Oscar and Esme). Thankfully, Ady had leapt on board with my challenge, and has arranged for his usual support crew to get involved. As I got ready to leave for Guernsey, I'd felt a bit like I was preparing for a job interview and could only hope that I wouldn't embarrass myself so much with my lack of experience that the team wanted nothing to do with me afterwards.

The day after I arrive, Ady gives me a tour of the island. Seeing a place you've studied relentlessly on a map in person for the first time is, without a doubt, a huge adventure milestone. In the case of Guernsey, it is a milestone that makes me feel a little bit sick—partly with excitement, partly because as I look down from the cliffs onto the sea I'd be kayaking and, more importantly, swimming in, waves are violently crashing on the rocks below. As we explore some more of Guernsey, I calm my anxiety by soaking up some of the natural beauty of the island. All the same, I quietly promise myself to prioritise open water training going forward.

Adrian and Andy have generously organised a magnificent dinner at their house in the evening, so I can meet the support crew and some more of the local open water swimming community— an impressive gang in their own right!

It's hugely reassuring and inspiring to hear their incredible tales of endurance and take in some of their advice. As an added bonus, it's all intertwined with the sort of hysterical laughter that happens when you instantly connect with people. By the end of the night, we are all friends, and being surrounded by such a warm hearted and determined bunch removes any doubts at all that I am in safe hands.

The next day is Valentine's Day, and it begins with an appropriately romantic little swim, Guernsey style, in the absolutely gorgeous but bitterly cold open water bathing pools. As an extra treat, it's raining heavily and I am already shivering as we walk from the changing room to the pool, into which the ocean waves regularly crash, so even this small, sectioned off part of the sea looks wild, inhospitable and intimidating.

On the count of three, we all dive in. The temperature of the water is a bracing nine degrees Celsius, and I instantly feel my skin scream in protest at the icy submersion. I tell myself to keep moving so I will warm up, and hear Ady shouting above the roar of the waves, telling me to focus on slowing down my breathing—I hadn't even realised it but my breathing cycle is incredibly short and quick due to the shock of the cold! Concentrating on this is the perfect distraction from the temperature, and as I slow down my breathing, I also slow down my panic.

I don't think I survive more than 15 minutes before having to get out. Ady makes sure to heartily congratulate me all the same . . . and then gets back in to swim some more. Back in the changing rooms, my frozen fingers make getting changed a very clumsy and awkward affair. I promise myself once more that I will prioritise those cold water swims I'd been meaning to do to acclimatise.

More Guernsey hospitality follows that night, and we

go round to a friend of Ady's to watch a rugby match. I am instantly welcomed in as one of the family yet again. Snacks turn into dinner, which then turns into the most brilliantly bizarre evening of dancing – complete with disco lights and smoke machine! A notable highlight is when the host – a local policeman – suddenly reappears in a glorious red Elvis skin suit and luscious black Elvis wig. Whatever apprehension I'd felt flying into Guernsey on Friday is long gone now, and I don't stop smiling all night. Guernsey – home of legends.

A short ferry ride from Guernsey is the island of Sark, the island I am planning to swim around. This is the section I am most worried about and, as I get ready to board the 8am ferry the next day, a knot of excitement in my stomach gnaws away at me, leaving me feeling mildly sick with anxiety. This mild nausea is soon made much worse by a very turbulent sea. Damn seasickness *again*. I spend the entire journey outside on the deck of the small ferry boat, getting thrashed by the wind and frequently smacked by the waves crashing over, but unable to go inside for fear I'll end up vomiting. Thankfully, I'm not actually sick but I am completely dishevelled by the time we come into the harbour at Sark. My appearance causes one woman waiting to board to nervously ask, 'Choppy crossing, was it?' It's written all over me – I clearly look every bit as rough as I feel.

I dry off with a cup of tea in a local café, and the seasickness soon fades away. It's time to explore the island. No cars are allowed on Sark so it's like stepping back in time. The only other traffic on the roads are leisurely cyclists and the occasional tractor – my favourite has 'DoCToR' as its number plate.

Hiking up to get a better view of the sea and to scout

potential public viewing points for the day of the swim, I am instantly reminded of the scale of the challenge. As the waves violently crash into the rocks below, I shudder. What have I taken on? The distances of the Channel Islands Triathlon (a 5 mile swim around sark, a 28 mile kayak around Guernsey and a 45 mile cycle around Jersey) are much less than those I'd previously considered for challenges and this had made me complacent. Seeing things up close has changed that in an instant. I quietly steel myself for a tough ride.

THE NEXT FOUR months were spent swimming weekly in the Royal Docks of East London. Face down into the cold, murky water with no views to distract me, for hours at a time – I often pondered that the biggest challenge of swimming might actually be boredom. My brain would eventually settle and usually after the first 30 minutes, the rest of the session would become almost meditative. I played the Alphabet Game – going through various categories in an attempt to distract my mind from the monotony and cold.

Countries:

A – Australia, Afghanistan, Argentina, Albania, Algeria, Angola

B – Belgium, Belize, Bangladesh, Bahrain

And so it would continue, for hours at a time. The best bit of every swim training session was afterwards, when I could drink a hot chocolate from my flask and snuggle into my DryRobe – a large adventure dressing gown, of sorts, which was lined in soft fleece and had a waterproof exterior. It was both my very own shelter and changing room all at once. Hot chocolate earned is a hot chocolate you really, really appreciate.

Alongside the swimming sessions, I'd also complete weekly strength sessions in the gym and substitute an indoor rowing machine for kayaking preparation, as it often wasn't practical time wise to pack up my kayak and head to a river. I also tried to get out on my bike every week but this was the section I was most confident about, so I firmly prioritised training for the other two disciplines. I reasoned I'd be able to rely on muscle memory and a generally good base level of fitness to complete the cycle around Jersey.

I'd partnered with the tourism boards of all three Channel Islands for the challenge so when the weekend did finally arrive, my team and I were thoroughly supported. The tourism boards had booked all of our ferries and arranged our accommodation, as well as covering the cost of our travel expenses for the weekend. I'd brought a talented and brilliant young filmmaker, Ben Arthur, with me to help capture the story. Ben's talent for photography and film-making is only matched by his warm, generous, ever-positive and kind nature – I couldn't have asked for a better person on the team.

ON THURSDAY 10 JUNE, we leave home at 4am, the sun rising behind us as we drive our rental van towards Poole and the ferry. We arrive into Guernsey later that afternoon. I have just enough time to have a quick shower and try to make myself look considerably less tired than I am feeling for the official press photos and interviews that the tourism board has lined up. The challenge is due to start the next day. My nerves are at an all-time high and the genuine excitement is tinged with an overwhelming sense of pressure. I wish I'd made more of an effort to swim in open water, but there just hasn't been enough time amidst everything else. That same old question reared its ugly head right on cue: what if I failed?

I don't sleep well that night, as that familiar doubt churns over and over. I'm also dreading the ferry ride to Sark – any bout of sea sickness will leave me in a dreadful state to begin. As it turns out, the Adventure Gods have smiled on us and we are greeted the next morning by bright skies and smooth seas. It's perfect.

As I step off the ferry in Sark on Friday morning, I am met by local adventure guide Budgie. Budgie has not only helped design the route, he's also going to be my support kayaker for the day. This is the first time we'd met in person but, as it seemed with all people on the Channel Islands, we are instant friends.

We tie Budgie's kayak behind the support boat with some rope and, a short ride later, we are at another harbour, Havre Gosselin, where today's swim would begin. Feeling better for having met my swim crew, I jump up to the steps of the harbour to change out of my cosy hoody and fleecy tracksuit bottoms and wiggle into my wetsuit. More nerves dissipated when I see Ady's smiling face on another boat waving at me. Although usually fiercely independent, I'm really glad he'll be with me in the water today. I hastily glug down a few sips of my homemade energy drink – coconut water with chia seeds – and neck a couple of spirulina tablets for an extra boost. I then pull on my neoprene boots, pull down my swimming cap and then finally pull on my neoprene gloves. I like to think I am, effectively, dressed like a neoprene ninja. Meanwhile, Ady waits patiently for me to stop faffing. I take a deep breath in as I sit on the side of the boat; I adjust my swimming cap one more time. I don't feel ready but it's time to jump in anyway.

Hilariously, my goggles leak within the first ten minutes – effectively blinding me. Ady, being the consummate professional, kindly gives me one of his spare pairs. After the initial hiccup, the first few hours go surprisingly quickly, and I begin to think I'd been worrying about nothing. The water is a comparatively pleasant 14 degrees – considerably warmer than it was for many of my training sessions. As time goes on, however, I start to feel chilly. My feeding sessions are scheduled for every 30 minutes – the idea being to supply me with regular energy to help keep me warm – but, as my appetite wanes, I am burning more calories than I am replacing, which means my body can't produce enough heat. I take to regularly slurping down hot chocolate from my flask during my feeding sessions, in addition to the pouches of baby food I've included as part of my nutrition strategy. The pouches don't contain sufficient calories by themselves, but they have the notable advantage of being liquified and therefore easier to digest. I'd thrown in some extra baby food just before leaving that morning, which proves to be a good decision, because after a couple of hours, I can't stomach anything else – least of all the many dry cereal-based energy bars I'd bought in bulk from the wholesale supermarket Costco because they were so cheap.

Not being used to swimming in waves, I'm also unintentionally regularly ingesting quite a lot of sea water as I turn my head to breathe. Two hours in, and the copious amounts of salt water mixed with the hot chocolate, combined with the mild sea sickness I'm beginning to feel – results in a molotov cocktail of nausea. The remaining hour in the water is nothing short of absolute hell. I swim two strokes, pause to retch – although never actually being sick – and then repeat.

It's at precisely this point that the local ITV news crew shows up. Budgie guides me behind some boats so I can have a retching session away from the cameras and then we carry on. My simple mantra of 'Just keep swimming, just keep swimming' has turned into 'Don't be sick, don't be sick'. I can't afford to lose the calories, so if my sea sickness gets much worse, it'll be game over.

I burn with envy for everyone on the support boats chatting away to each other and taking in the beautiful sights of Sark – all I can see is glimpses of the sky and the same murky turquoise shade of sea water, and the occasional jellyfish that I try to telepathically plead with to leave me alone. I'm finding it almost impossible to distract myself from the misery – whatever peaceful meditative states I'd found during training are nowhere to be seen now. This feels like torture.

I'm within sight of the harbour but I don't feel like I can make it. Desperately I try to hold onto some nearby rocks so I can violently retch some more. Every time the sea water hits my throat, I am gagging as a reflex to ingesting too much salt. It feels impossible to carry on. Who the hell invited Chunder Dragon to the party?!

Ady and the support crew jump into action, shouting words of encouragement. Despite my slower time and near-constant faffing inevitably causing Ady his own issues – while I'm in a wetsuit, he's just in a pair of swimming shorts with some vaseline smeared on for added protection – he remains a strong and encouraging figure.

'Leave your mark on Sark,' jokes Budgie, as I heave helplessly on the rocks.

'That's it,' says Ady, pointing to the tantalisingly close harbour. 'That's all you've gotta do.'

Before I know it, Amanda, one of Ady's crew that I'd met at the dinner a couple of months ago, and an accomplished open water swimmer in her own right, has jumped into the water. (I like to think that Amanda always has a swimming costume on underneath her clothes, much like Clark Kent is always ready to transform into Superman.)

I am flanked by Ady to my left and Amanda on my right, and in this formation we begin the final push to the harbour together. Swim, swim, retch, swim, swim, retch. Just keep going. There's a constant roar of encouragement coming from both support boats and from the people in the harbour. Each time I look up and see Ady and Amanda next to me, it's all the comfort I need. I absorb their energy; I felt them willing me to succeed and know I can't let them down. We're a team now and we can't fail.

Finally reaching the steps of the harbour, I am greeted by huge applause from the locals, many of whom have been tracking my progress all day courtesy of my online tracker map. Clambering up to the port, I am shivering uncontrollably and I vow never to do anything so stupid ever again. I am still a total mess – goggle lines firmly imprinted on to my face and visibly shaking as my team help me into my DryRobe – when the film crew for the local news arrives for an interview.

Meanwhile, Ady looks as fresh as a daisy and doesn't seem at all tired, or even slightly cold, as he cheerfully stands in his bright red swimming trunks next to me. If Ady wasn't so entirely lovable I would have found this irritating, but as he envelops me in a bear hug and congratulates me, I'm just grateful that he was part of today's incredible team. Ady's training to complete seven ocean swims – the next of which will be a much bigger and much tougher ocean swim, the Molokai straight: 26 miles from Moloaki to Oahu in Hawaii – and while our swim around Sark is a monumental feat for me, it's simply a good training swim for Ady. So there's no doubt that he could have finished the swim quicker without me, but that doesn't stop him from heartily congratulating me several times on the achievement. Once more, I feel humbled by the team I've found myself surrounded by and hugely inspired by Ady's gentle grace and unwavering support throughout the day.

That night, I feel like I've been beaten up – every muscle aches. Having never swum in saltwater for any length of time before, I also hadn't anticipated the need to put Vaseline around my neck – which rubbed against the wetsuit every time I turned my head to breathe. The resulting chafing mark on my neck resembles some kind of werewolf attack, which makes for a very emotional experience in the shower. As I sink into bed and feel myself almost immediately drifting off to sleep, I feel proud but, more than that, I feel relieved that I hadn't failed. Swimming was always the section I was most apprehensive about. One down, two more to go.

THE NEXT DAY, we are greeted by ominous thick fog and rain as I assemble Ariel on the beach in Guernsey. The weather is due to further worsen later in the day, with winds reaching 30–40 knots. With 28 miles ahead of us today, all I can do is get an early start and hope for the best.

I'm joined for the day by more friendly locals: Daniel is going to be in the support boat with Ben and Paul is going to kayak next to me. Together, Paul and I paddle out through the peaceful stillness of the morning and past the barely visible cliffs, the eerie silence broken up by the occasional blast of a fog horn. I can just about see my paddling partner through the fog and it takes the support boat a while to find us, even with my tracking device. The waves continue to roll around us – we vanish and reappear to each other as our comparatively tiny kayaks rise and fall with the waves.

I am, quite literally, out of my depth. It feels like paddling on a bucking bronco and, for the first time ever, I start to feel seasick in my kayak. Paul isn't faring much better. It's a humbling experience, to be thrashed around in the almighty ocean, and one I half-relish and half-resent. Having only ever paddled in rivers before, it's as exhilarating as it is terrifying. As the winds pick up and the conditions continue to worsen, it leans considerably more towards the terrifying end of the scale. We manage to pull into a nearby bay and assess the situation.

I know as I approach the bay that it's not safe to paddle in conditions like this. The weather warnings coming in on the radio confirm it and my paddling partner gracefully bows out. The next section, around the north of the island, is too rocky for the support boat to accompany me, so should anything happen, I'd be completely by myself and in very difficult conditions. The risk is too high and I can't justify it. The local coastguards and RNLI have their hands full as it is, I don't want to add to their burdens just by being an obstinate idiot. I reluctantly pack up Ariel, doing my best to remain outwardly cheerful to the crew but inwardly sulking – I'm acutely aware of a second public kayaking mishap. Although I know I've yet again made the right decision, it stings. Stubbornness kicks in again and, with the ever-cheerful Ben by my side, we decide to finish the loop of the island on foot, walking a half marathon and eventually returning to the bay from which I started out from at 7pm – 12 hours after leaving.

All I really want to do that night is sulk some more and stew over another paddling related failure, but Ady and Andy have other plans. They arrive at the holiday cottage basecamp armed with a gigantic feast of Indian takeaway. Over dinner, Ady's own tales of mishaps and incredible endeavours lessen the sting of today's premature retreat from the water and I soon find myself laughing again. Understanding completely the physical fatigue of the challenge and satisfied that I can't eat anymore, ady and Andy quickly retreat so that I can get some sleep. I hug them goodbye and, for the second time in as many days, I silently thank the universe for sending Ady and Andy into my life.

THE NEXT DAY is the final day of the challenge and sees a visit to the third island – Jersey. The ferry over is delayed so I have less than two hours to check in to the apartment kindly provided by the Jersey tourism board, hastily eat a huge plate of pasta and then change into my cycling gear – feeling like I probably ate a bit too much pasta as the lycra now seemed a tad tighter than usual.

I'd put an invite out for any local Jersey cyclists to join me for the final leg of the triathlon. Nervously making my way to the meeting point with slightly tired legs from the impromptu wander around Guernsey the day before, I wonder if anyone was coming to my party. One by one, they turn up; eight of them all armed with a smile and lots of Haribo. With this much sugar, we're clearly going to be fine! Heading up the team is James Walker from the Jersey tourism board – a friendly chap I'd spoken to a great deal on the phone. It was lovely to meet him in person and I was grateful that he'd be joining the ride, too. The Channel Islands hospitality shines through once more.

Jersey throws all possible weather conditions at us: wind, rain, thick grey clouds and blazing hot sunshine. It doesn't seem to matter one bit – our mini peloton is flying along regardless. James and the rest of the local cyclists each take it in turn to lead and I get a crash course in group riding. One notable benefit is that I get shielded from the strong headwind now developing. Each member of the group also takes it in turns to ride alongside me, and as we chat and laugh away, I'm thankfully distracted from the weary, dull ache developing in my legs.

All the while, Ben is zooming along in the rental van, playing an elaborate game of tag around the island, trying to capture video footage for the mini film I'm making for the tourism board, whilst also trying not to annoy the other traffic too much. Frequently he goes ahead to scout a good angle and then waits for us to pass. Obviously, not knowing when and where he will pop up next makes it tricky to look as cool as possible for the film. I turn one corner with my face jammed so full of sweets that my cheeks are bulging – not unlike a hamster – to find Ben cheerfully waiting and asking me to say hello to the camera. I wave and do my best to slim down my sweet filled face. When Ben will go to edit this section he'll think I'm poking my tongue out at him – only to realise that in actual fact, I am mid-scoff and have a Percy Pig between my teeth.

Thanks to the wonderful gang that I have with me for the day, the hours soon fly by and, before I know it, we are approaching the final section with the clock tower in Saint Helier where the day started in sight. As with all challenges, no matter how small, the finish line is a moment to savour. I start to run over what I will say to the group when we finish; how I'm so grateful for all of the local hospitality that I've received through this challenge, how I've fallen in love with the Channel Islands, how I've realised the phenomenal power of community to make a difference and how there is such merit in smaller adventures that you can pack into a weekend. What came out when Ben asked me how I was feeling, video camera in hand, was significantly less grandiose: 'Today was such a good day. I'm so happy. I didn't think anyone was going to turn up! ALL the pizza! ALL the ice cream!'

After exchanging several sweaty hugs with my new Jersey friends, I head back to the apartment where the team and I do in fact eat a celebratory meal of greasy takeaway pizza. Jersey has some incredible restaurants but after endurance challenges, I will choose victory pizza every single time.

AFTER WORKING SO HARD PULLING TOGETHER the many, many logistics for the Channel Islands Triathlon, it was a struggle to accept that it was all over so quickly. I felt lost. In many ways, my weekend adventure had been an experiment. I wanted to show that you didn't have to go far away or disappear for months to have a great adventure. I wanted to make adventure seem more accessible by focusing on adventures that anyone could do, regardless of family commitments or annual leave. It had been such a huge success that I decided to see if I could develop this further. So, as I made plans for 2017, I considered other mini adventures that I could do to show people just how attainable both adventure and exercise could be.

As part of this, I focused on leading free outdoor fitness sessions with KEEN all throughout the UK. I consider the outdoors to be one big fitness playground and I wanted to show others the potential, too. With gym memberships getting more expensive and lives getting ever busier, I wanted to show that you don't need much time or any fancy equipment to keep fit. The humble park bench, for example, can be used for split lunges, tricep dips and incline press-ups. Steps are perfect for building up the strength needed to tackle hills, with no hills in sight! Use what you have – start where you are.

Touching upon the subject of time, now seems like a good opportunity to mention that the average person in Britain apparently watches a staggering 27 hours of television each week. That's ten years over a lifetime! I opted out of having a TV years ago, but if that's too extreme, perhaps consider that cutting out even an hour of TV each day would amount to two weeks of extra time over the course of a year. Plenty of time to get in some exercise and plan that adventure!

As a top priority, I also wanted to show people that keeping fit could be fun – fun was at the heart of all of the TrailFit sessions. Putting my previous experience as a personal trainer to good use, I designed the sessions to make people sweat, sure, but also to make people smile. It upsets me that people view exercise as some sort of punishment; I always think they just haven't found the right sport. There's such joy to be found in moving your body.

In amidst the community events, I also organised some more smaller challenges with friends – like cycling overnight to Paris, a challenge I affectionately named Pedalling for Patisserie. There were ten of us all together for that one: we met at London's Greenwich Park at 5pm with the aim of getting to the Eiffel Tower within 24 hours.

A couple of months later, I also cycled overnight to Holland, similarly named Pedalling for Pancakes, with my friends Elise Downing and Kate Davis. These mini adventures were rewarding in their own way but I still wanted one challenge for me. A challenge that would hit that need of mine to feel completely out of my depth and really excited, as well as give me the opportunity to grow and evolve.

5 THERE'S MAGIC IN MISERY

'Somewhere along the line we seem to have confused comfort with happiness. Dostoyevsky had it right: "Suffering is the sole origin of consciousness." Never are my senses more engaged than when the pain sets in. There is a magic in misery. Just ask any runner'
– Dean Karnazes

For as long as I can remember, I have truly detested running. In my early twenties, I used to do it as a form of masochistic punishment every now and then when I felt like I'd overindulged, but I never did it regularly. I would always think, roughly four minutes in, 'Why on earth would anyone do this?! It's awful!' I expect part of the issue was that I'd fallen in love with cycling from the moment I had my first bike as a child and by comparison, running just seemed so much slower and . . . well, pointless.

That was all well and good but I considered that this

dislike of running had turned into something far more unacceptable – I had told myself I couldn't run. I'd decided that I wasn't a runner and that I couldn't do it; I didn't have the right genetic make up. The only affinity I had to running was with the Bruce Springsteen song 'Born to Run' which I absolutely love and would often play at full volume on repeat. But actual running? No thanks.

Throughout every public talk I gave, there was a nagging awareness that I was being rather hypocritical. There I was on stages, all over Europe, telling people to defy their limits and that they were more powerful than they could dream of – all the while with the little caveat in my own mind of 'unless it comes to running, which of course I am utterly incapable of'. It was time to take some of my own medicine.

I could have tackled my running demons in a reasonable and logical fashion, perhaps going through a 5k, 10k, half marathon, and maybe eventually leading up to a full marathon. But that didn't motivate or excite me in the slightest. Instead, I decided to settle on the much more exciting figure of . . . 100 miles. If I was going to run, I wanted to become a centurion – after all, doesn't the word centurion just sound so much cooler?!

I had, by now, developed two criteria each endurance challenge:

It must take me somewhere new, so the journey is an exploration.

It must push me – I must have to really reach and dig deep for it, usually finding it completely overwhelming at some point. Basically, success cannot be guaranteed.

With that in mind, I decided that it might be fun to run across an island. I loved the idea of having another self-contained island adventure, just like I had on the Channel

Islands, and so I began researching different islands that might be a good candidate. I also convinced my friend Tessa Jennett to join me. Tessa is a really strong runner and I'd hoped that I might pick up some of her ability by osmosis.

Sat in a café overlooking Tower Bridge with Tessa, googling away fuelled by coffee, I discovered on Wikipedia that the island of Fuerteventura was not only 100 miles in length, but it also apparently translated to 'strong adventure'. We took this as an excellent sign and decided immediately that this was the island for us. As luck would have it, a long distance hiking trail, the GR131, went straight across the island so it didn't seem like we needed to do much route planning either. As further research, I bought a guidebook – that I briefly flicked through and then promptly put back in my drawer, until it was time for the challenge to begin. The idea was that we could combine two hiking days into one running day – as we'd theoretically be going quicker – and complete the challenge in four days, instead of the recommended eight days mentioned in the guidebook. Simple!

I knew that, of all the challenges I'd taken on so far, this was the one most likely to make me grumpy. I was aiming to break a lifelong habit of running avoidance and I decided that I needed to enlist some help.

This came in the form of the Running School in London and the Altitude Centre situated next door. I am so grateful to Mike and Nick at the Running School for supporting me to begin with –especially after I turned up for our first meeting and confessed that the longest I'd ever run up to this point was five kilometres, and even that was not something I tried to do with any regularity. Enthusiastically, I'd then followed this confession with 'But I do lots of cycling! So perhaps that helps?' Mike's expression was somewhere between amusement and horror, with a definite smirk lurking, as he simply replied, 'No, it doesn't.'

Week after week, I hit the treadmill at the Running School, under close supervision of Nick. It turned out that due to being much more of a cyclist, I had over-dominant quads and somewhat lazy glutes. It's a common enough problem, but one I would really need to address, as over such a long distance it had huge implications for efficient technique and also, most importantly, injury avoidance. I wasn't overly concerned about speed, but I did care about making sure I was physically able to complete the challenge without causing long term damage to my body.

Each week, Nick went through a set of pre-running exercises designed to fire up my lazy glutes before getting me to run on the treadmill at various speeds and inclines, all the while filming me so he could point out various tweaks that I needed to make to improve my technique.

I reintroduced kettlebells back into my training sessions on a weekly basis – aiming to not only strengthen my glutes but improve the posterior kinetic chain (i.e. the muscles on the back of the body) as a whole. I also made sure to regularly dig into some of my muscle kinks and release them with the help of a foam roller and a lacrosse ball. The official term for this process is 'self-myofascial relief'; the unofficial term is 'torture' – albeit of a strangely enjoyable hurts-so-good kind. Strength and conditioning work often gets neglected, but it's essential to have solid base on which to build miles from – a strong athlete is an injury resistant athlete. Slowly but surely, my heavy shuffle turned into more of a functional and lighter-footed gait. I was still no gazelle but at least I was less of an elephant.

I combined my weekly sessions at the Running School with 30-minute sessions on another treadmill in the Altitude Centre's chamber next door. I began to both loathe and love my training days here. The altitude chamber was set to stimulate 2,710 metres – 15 per cent oxygen. My lungs would scream at me throughout each session, feeling like an 80-year-old grandmother who'd been chain smoking her entire life. But then the sessions would end and I'd feel full of endorphins. It was addictive.

Between the two of them, I gradually began to feel like I might be able to run after all. The more efficient I became, the further I could run and this became the key to unlocking running for me – exploring. I spent long afternoons seeking out new trails and exploring places I simply wouldn't be able to reach with my road bike. When a niggle in my calf meant that I had to take a couple of weeks off running I found that I actually missed it. For the first time in my life, I considered that maybe runners weren't such a crazy bunch after all. However, this was a conclusion I almost immediately took back after the challenge began.

WE ARE ABOUT 30 minutes into day one of the challenge and we have come to realise that just because a path is suitable for hiking, it doesn't mean it's ideal for running. This is going to be a lot tougher than we thought.

Not only had I completely underestimated the terrain, I hadn't factored in the effect of running in 34-degree heat. Even though we set our alarm for 4am, it feels like no time at all before the heat kicks in. And when it does, it's suffocating and unbearable.

After completing the first half of the first day, Tessa and I seek out a local café where we both devour a cold can of life-giving Orange Fanta and brace ourselves for a rough few days. The rest of the day is fuelled by excitement. We may have signed ourselves up for a lot of pain, but the challenge had begun! One of the reasons I steer away from organised events is that I absolutely love seeing a unique challenge that I've dreamt up come to life. We finished the day in high spirits. One marathon down, only three more to go!

The next day, we again begin in darkness, with the sun slowly rising as we run through the desert. Clambering up and down sand dunes, we are moving slowly, but at least we're moving. Then, a few hours into our slow but determined battle against the sand, having not seeing another soul all morning and with no sign of civilisation within sight, out of nowhere we encounter a security guard. Quite exactly what he can possibly be guarding out there we can't work out. The language barrier makes things a little confusing, but one thing is for sure, we are not allowed to go any further. This our friendly security guard makes clear through a comedy game of charades. –He does an impression of running with his fingers across his palm and them immediately wags a strong finger, saying 'No, no!' This much we understand perfectly.

It turns out that the harsh landscape of Fuerteventura is the perfect place to replicate unforgiving alien lands and we are not allowed anywhere near the 'set' of a science fiction film currently being filmed there. Despite our protests and attempts to explain our challenge, in a language he can't understand, we are bundled into his car and driven back a few kilometres – our hard-earned progress of the morning erased in minutes. Dropping us off at a distance he deemed safe, he says we will have to make our way back to the road – roughly, he says, a mile away.

It's not a mile away. So often people in cars seem to be

oblivious, despite their good intentions, of actual distances. It takes us hours to reach the road. Encountering a few animal bones along the way, Tessa and I soon descend into hysterics, desperately staving off our bad moods by cursing the perfectly charming and affable security guard and doing our best David Attenborough impressions, animal skull in hand, to narrate the ridiculous situation:

'Here, we see the remains of what once would have been a mighty beast – struck down in its prime – by the harsh and unforgiving lands of Fuerteventura and the merciless security guards that protect them. Whilst foraging for water, this poor wretched creature eventually succumbed to dehydration and died a slow and lonely death – the additional 300 miles [we were feeling dramatic] he was forced to march in the relentless heat proving, alas, to be a challenge he would not – he could not – survive.'

Unable to run along the trail and unwilling to run along the busy motorway, we call our friend David Altabev for an early pick up. David, a photographer, has joined us for the week to act as support car (dropping us off and picking us up at the beginning and end of each day) and also to help capture the adventure, building up his own photography portfolio. Having covered the equivalent distance for the first half of the day, albeit in the wrong direction, we restock with water, empty the sand from our shoes and immediately begin on the second section for the day, hoping to run off the frustrations of the morning.

The second stage starts innocently enough. Gravelly, hilly—what we'd come to expect by now – and we cheerfully make our way up, up, up, holding to the consolation prize of 'slow progress is better than no progress'. Although we seem to be continuously climbing uphill, we're also being treated to exceptional sweeping views of the landscape which, when we wipe the sweat away from our eyes so we can see, makes it seem worthwhile.

Still upwards we climb. The hours pass, and our progress is excruciatingly slow.

As afternoon slips into early evening, and we are high up in the remote mountains with the wind blowing fiercely, a quiet concern begins to emerge. At 5pm, we find ourselves on top of a ridgeline with steep descents that don't look at all appealing, and our concern comes into full focus. This is not a good place to be with evening approaching. We make the decision to backtrack for the second time that day and head down towards the nearest road, very slowly picking our way down the unforgiving slope, my stomach flipping every time my foot slips and skids on the steep terrain.

Truth be told, although I'm generally fine with heights and in a perverse way I quite enjoy the thrill of being up high, scrambling on scree terrifies me. Each and every set of rocks that crumbles underneath my tentative footing and tumbles down the mountain causes my stomach to leap into my throat. My movements got slower and slower – in fact, I'm getting more and more scared to move by the second. I understand that fear serves a purpose but in situations like this, feeling like a frozen deer in headlights is just not practical. There is no other way to get off the mountain and it is of course my own fault for getting up there in the first place, so I'm just going to have to find a way to cope with the increasing levels of panic now building.

'I said don't worry . . . about a thing.' My voice nervously trembles. 'Every little thing, is gonna be all . . . riiight.' This seems like exactly the opportune moment to start singing Bob Marley, a tactic I often employ when I need reassurance.

I have great faith that if I just keep singing these

affirming lyrics, everything really would be all right. At that moment, though, I can't remember many of the other lyrics, or indeed any other song, so poor Tessa is subjected to me singing those same lines over and over again, getting steadily louder in defiance of my fear – as if I somehow think I can quite literally drown it out – as we slowly make our way down.

Tessa, being a hardy Scottish lass well accustomed to exploring the mountains of Scotland, is faring much better than me. In fact, much to my frustration, she seems to have very successfully channelled her inner mountain goat brilliantly, whereas the only creature I've apparently managed to channel was a very nervous, and possibly drunk, baby giraffe who hadn't yet mastered the art of walking at all, let alone scrambling. At times, as we clutch desperately onto a very sketchy iron barbed fence loosely dug into the ground, or just go down as best as we can at an angle to the slope, I curse every life decision that has brought me to this point.

When we eventually reach the road again, relief floods over us and hysterical laughter once again returns. I kneel down and kissed the dusty tarmac. The day had begun at 5am and it is 7:30pm by the time we get back to our apartment, mentally and physically drained, more than a little humbled and very happy to be back down from the mountain.

The next day, the alarm goes off at 4am but I feel broken. Somewhat in awe of the damage that can be done in two days, I have one thought playing over and over again in my head – 'I can't do this. It's impossible – I physically can't do this.'

My legs feel like they have been filled with lead overnight. Heavy and with a dull, enduring ache, they feel too heavy to move. The real issue, however, is my feet – they are in tatters and barely recognisable. The thought of forcing my blister-covered skin back into trainers for another day of agony is an unbearable thought. Each step causes pain. Every doubt I've ever had about being a runner is playing like an orchestra in my head now, like a symphony of sabotage. I shouldn't have done this – I'm not a runner.

I get ready anyway because I can't bring myself to tell Tessa and David how incapable I feel. Being the only one here who supposedly makes a living out of endurance challenges, I'm embarrassed to admit just how broken I am and I can't gather up the courage to tell them that I think we need to add an extra day to the challenge.

Quietly, I begin to tape up my feet and accept that I'm about to fail again. I cynically muse that I'm going to give people a whole new disaster to talk about. I'll go as far as I can, I think, but there's no way I'll be hitting today's daily target. My tank feels completely empty.

Step by step, just keep moving. It's all I focus on. As we get into the morning's section, I confide to Tessa that I don't think I'll be able to do the full distance today. Understanding completely, she nonetheless encourages me to just focus on this section first and tells me we can reassess the remaining mileage later. Breaking huge challenges down into bite-size chunks is advice I often give in my talks so I smile when she repeats it back to me. We all need a little reminder sometimes.

It's a good strategy. Much to my surprise, the first section of the day goes quicker than expected and I emerge from my pain cave feeling triumphant. I may not have yet won the war, but I have won this battle. Naturally, this calls for a celebration, and in addition to our daily Orange Fanta, Tessa and I decide to order a gigantic ice cream sundae. I think ice cream is possibly one of mankind's greatest inventions. I actually consider it to be a really efficient fuel for endurance challenges – full of fat and sugar – but on a far less scientific level, it always makes me really happy.

Fuelled by our tower of ice cream, the second half of the day is unrecognisable from the sombre mood of the morning. The terrain is also kinder, so whilst progress isn't exactly at record breaking pace it is consistent – which in itself does wonders for morale. Despite spending most of the day feeling like it was going to be impossible, we complete the full distance. After inhaling a gigantic mound of pasta for dinner, and also the standard tin of pineapple for dessert (pineapple is anti-inflammatory – really handy to know for endurance challenges!), I happily collapse into the bed of our rented apartment at the end of day three.

It's 4am on day four and the inexhaustible army of self doubt is awake and thriving before I've even sat up in bed. It's the final day of the challenge but, once again, I'm not convinced I have it in me to hit the full distance for the day. My weary body is full of aches and weighed down by sheer dread of the pain still yet to come. I feel like a complete idiot for taking on this challenge in the first place. In many ways, I am an idiot. But I'm also a very stubborn idiot.

The morning is fuelled by sheer bloody-minded determination. I also get quite philosophical and muse on a quote by Japanese author Huruki Murakami – 'Pain is inevitable, but suffering is optional.'

I do my best to come to a zen like acceptance that the next few hours are just really, really going to hurt – and that this is totally fine. It's an effective strategy and with 11 miles down, we have reached the halfway point for the day. I'm amazed once more at the abuse my body will tolerate – and I quietly ask it to please tolerate just a little bit more.

Our snack break contains a potent mix of café con leche (condensed milk combined with coffee and topped up with hot milk – sweet, delicious and perfect fuel for energy depleted runners!) and ibuprofen—whatever it takes. Onwards we go, with a relatively small but still somewhat overwhelming figure of 15 final miles to go. Each step brings us closer; each step hurts— it's taking every bit of resolve we have to keep moving.

I'm not convinced I'm actually capable of hitting the final target until we're just three kilometres away, and then it suddenly begins to dawn on me that, despite wanting desperately to quit for two days and despite being in absolute agony, we're going to make it!

We run triumphantly into the town square in Corralejo and hug the sign that signifies the end of the route, and then each other, whilst David showers us in a bottle of prosecco he'd bought especially for this moment. Tessa and I then beeline for the sea. In an act of euphoric celebration, we take off our shoes and dive straight into the sea fully dressed. I am immediately reminded of the fact that my feet are riddled with blisters, many of them rubbed raw with painfully exposed skin which, when mixed with the salty sea water, brings tears to my eyes, but this isn't a moment I would change for the world. A feeling of contentment settles over me and, at long last, a few inner demons have been silenced. There really is magic in misery.

ARRIVING BACK FROM FUERTEVENTURA, I only had a couple of days to 'recover' before I'm once again diving head first into talks and community fitness sessions all over the UK. For all the preparation that has gone into

Fuerteventura, it was once again over too quickly and the sharp return to reality took some getting used to.

However, in addition to a couple of smaller challenges peppered in between, I still had one more adventure up my sleeve before the year ends – Scotland's North Coast 500 route. Starting and ending in Inverness, the NC500 is a 516 mile coastal lap around the stunning highlands of Scotland. I'd been aware of this route ever since completing the Wild Atlantic Way in Ireland in 2015 and I'd decided it was time to get back to another simple and self-supported challenge – no photographers/videographers, no support drivers, just me and my bike Dory. With such warm memories of Ireland, I couldn't wait to strip everything back and quieten down the noise of everyday life again.

It felt right to be stepping back into self-supported challenges – to be taking some time out to evaluate where I was and where I was headed. These shorter challenges had been fun and I loved that I'd shown how accessible adventures could be, but they weren't really where I'd seen myself headed on a long term basis. I'd been so busy cramming in challenges in an attempt to put some space between the failure of Russia, I hadn't really stopped long enough to consider any kind of plan – I just knew that I couldn't stand to stay still. Life on the run was no way to live. I decided eight days in Scotland was a perfect way to test the ground of solo travel once more.

6 DON'T LET THE GREMLIN DRIVE

*'Imperfections are not inadequacies; they are reminders that
we're all in this together'*
— Brené Brown

On 23 August 2017, I am on a sleeper train headed to Inverness. I sit on the bunk bed in my cabin with my head in my hands and tears cascading uncontrollably down my face. Just 24 hours before getting on the train, I'd been in Ireland – this time to attend my Nan's funeral.

I'd only seen Nan a handful of times since my uncle's wedding – the last visit was to her nursing home where Nan was, reluctantly, now a full time resident. There was no doubt that as her health deteriorated she needed full time care, but Nan was fiercely independent and struggled with life in the nursing home. The staff at the home were warm, kind and generous but my visit to Nan broke my heart. Her movement had become fairly restricted and, although she would sometimes venture into town for tea – often with my cousins when they visited – a small walk around the building, with Nan in a wheelchair, was as much as Nan felt like doing the day I went to see her with my mum.

I completely understood why she needed to be there, but her loneliness was palpable and it crushed me to think of her there, staring out of the window, waiting for visitors to brighten up the long, repetitive days. It was especially cruel that her own home, where Mum and I were staying for the weekend, was only a five-minute walk away – and yet it was a home Nan would never live in again.

Nan always loved hearing about my adventures and we spent a happy couple of hours going over my latest challenges. All weekend, she did her best to remain cheerful, as ever on a mission to constantly feed me, but it was an unmistakably tough existence for such a vibrant woman. Despite telling her not to get up, when it was time for Mum and me to leave Nan had stubbornly chased us in her own very slow but determined way, shuffling along with her walking frame down the hall to wave us off. Leaving was never going to be easy but that last image had haunted me ever since. Us leaving, her unable to. It felt cruel and unfair.

Returning to Ireland for the funeral, I realised that visits to Ireland would never be the same again. My grandparents had separated a few years ago and Grandad had moved back to England. Meeting my cousins at the airport, we all mused on how Nan was always the lynchpin for our visits. I had always loved visiting Ireland, and I think so much of what I'd loved about my ride across the west coast had been discovering the hidden pockets of the country that I'd heard my grandparents talk about. It just wasn't the same now. None of us could quite believe that she'd gone.

I'd flown out not only to say goodbye to Nan but also to

try and support Mum who, with both of my aunts, had spent the final few days with Nan. I've never been very good with bereavement (is anyone?!) and spent most of the time sobbing, despite wanting to be strong for Mum. I repeatedly wished my older brothers had been able to fly out – I thought they'd have probably been better at this than me. I had been just as bad when my Nanny Rose had passed away years before and I'd gone with my dad to help clear out her house in Frome, Somerset. Even then, although totally helpless to control my grief, I'd felt guilty for not being able to hold myself together a bit better and provide the support I desperately wanted to.

Each of the cousins had something to read for the service, as arranged by my mum and aunts. I was to read out a poem by Mary Elizabeth Frye, titled 'Do Not Stand at My Grave and Weep'. It's a beautiful poem but I couldn't get more than two lines into it before, in front of the packed church, I found myself ironically choking on the words through tears that I just couldn't hold back. As the only professional public speaker in the family, I wasn't doing a very good job.

My uncle rushed up to stand next to me, placing a steadying hand on my shoulder and holding my hand as I deeply inhaled and managed – just about – to finish the reading. I sat back down at the church pew and my nan's sister passed along some tissues, while my younger cousin, sat in the row behind me, placed another steadying hand on my shoulder. I silently thanked her and was grateful that she didn't take her hand off my shoulder until I'd managed to slow down my breathing once more and finally stop the flood of tears.

Irish funerals are intense but they are also founded on a strong sense of support. It was an open casket and as we sat around the chapel, people from all over – friends, relatives and fellow residents of the nursing home alike – walked around to say goodbye to Nan and to individually shake our hands and offer their condolences. At regular intervals, I considered how happy Nan would have been to have us all together, half expecting her to show up at some point because she would never miss a family gathering – and this would inevitably cause a few more tears. Throughout, I was humbled by the incredible sense of community in Ireland that once more shone through.

Now, a day later, having briefly returned home to pick up my bike, I don't feel even slightly ready to tackle the fierce Scottish mountains. Friends and family sensibly suggested I postpone, but blind stubbornness made this an impossible option for me. I irrationally felt I'd be letting down too many people by not going through with it. If I'm being really honest, I still had a Russia-shaped chip on my shoulder that meant that even the slightest hint of failure, of any kind – even a delay, would induce feelings of sheer, angry panic in me. I could stomach the failure of Russia, but apparently only on the condition that I never failed again. 'I don't tap out to tiredness', I reminded myself. I was going ahead, no matter what. eight days of hell, I thought. Then you can grieve. Then you can rest.

THE FIRST DAY sets the tone for the trip—setting off from Inverness with a target of 83 miles to get to Applecross, I'm greeted with a fierce headwind, frequent downpours and often hilly but consistently beautiful scenery. It's brutal—but gorgeous. I finish ten miles short of my target, exhausted but ever optimistic that my body would adapt, as it always does.

The next day is a little kinder, although the fickle weather continues to mock me – switching between blazing hot sunshine and heavy downpours. It seems that the quickest way to stop the rain is to actually put my waterproofs on and, similarly, removing the waterproofs seems to be a green light for the downpours to return immediately. All day this ridiculous game continues, so I am either soaking wet and shivering or boiling hot and stewing in sweat. Determined to remain in good spirits, I have to laugh. By the end of the day, I'm weary but hopeful that day three would be better. Then I come across 'Nan's Café' shortly before finishing for the day and I choke back a few tears. I really need to recharge; I haven't slept properly in days.

After loading up with a hearty dinner of scampi and chips at a nearby pub, I am drifting off to sleep in my tent by 9pm. A couple of hours later I wake up, hit by waves of nausea. Whatever I'd eaten has not agreed with me one bit, but I'm desperate not to lose vital calories. I sit up in my sleeping bag, inhaling deeply, sip some water and try to ignore the gurgling in my stomach, attempting to channel some kind of Jedi mind tricks over my digestive system. Unsurprisingly, this doesn't work and inevitably I am soon violently sick. Three more rounds of vomiting continue throughout the night and into the early hours of the morning. I eventually get back to sleep around 4am, then my alarm goes off a couple of hours later, signalling it's time to hit the road.

I feet like absolute hell. I'm utterly depleted, with puffy eyes stinging and a burning throat. Cycling a couple of miles down the road seems like a herculean feat, let alone covering the 90 miles I need to that day to stay on target.

But I'd said the challenge would take me seven days and blind determination once more means that I absolutely refuse to be flexible and deviate from this, considering it a huge failure if I were to come up short in any way. The return sleeper train ticket has been booked (and sponsored) and I refuse to change it to even one day later. So, I can't afford to do any less mileage today without making the days still to come absolutely horrendous. This is no terrain in which to be doing extra miles with a fully loaded bike.

Reluctantly and wearily, I begin. I feel like I am perpetually losing a fight with an angry gorilla, but I am moving forwards – albeit gradually – and sometimes that's all you need. After regularly snacking for a couple of hours, I'd managed to top up my calories and around midday I finally start to feel vaguely human again. There are no fun weather games today – just torrential rain with very few breaks in between the violent showers. I seem to be climbing uphill all day. Any time I stop to catch my breath or even to appreciate the views, I'm inevitably surrounded by swarms of midges. Hundreds of tiny, irritating, biting, invasive midges. I like to think they are there as a motivational nudge to keep me going because they make rest breaks so completely unbearable that I just stop taking them.

The rain has caused several small running channels of water to cover the roads and my cheap waterproofs are completely ineffective. Onwards and constantly upwards I heave my bike, shivering and constantly dreaming of one thing only: hot chocolate. I promise myself that when I do eventually finish this gruelling section, I will treat myself to a gigantic hot chocolate, topped with whipped cream and as many marshmallows as could fit in the huge mug. The obsession grows throughout the afternoon and I continue onwards like a vampire possessed with a chocolatey thirst. I grow ever more tired and, with my legs refusing to cycle uphill anymore, I end up pushing the bike up the last few steep sections of the day's route. My left leg is now twinging painfully, a feeling I dismiss as a niggle that will be better after a night's rest.

I usually console myself on adventures when I'm tired by appreciating the scenery and thinking how it would be a shame to travel through such stunning landscapes in a motorised vehicle – you pass by too quickly to really appreciate the views; you don't get to relish the downhill after working so hard to get to the top and you don't get to know intimately every curve of the horizon. On this day, however, I burn with envy at anyone in a car or, especially, a motorhome. I muse bitterly to myself that they'd have the heating on and the radio playing as they effortlessly covered vast distances, cosily cocooned from the elements. I try to consider that I have the moral upper ground here – my experience was definitely more 'character building' – but at this particular moment the moral high ground seems vastly overrated. I wonder if the passing vehicles felt sorry for me and, as I slowly trudged onwards, I fantasise about a kind driver pulling over with a flask of hot tea and some biscuits before perhaps offering me admiration and praise for my surely impressive display of resilience and tenacity. No one stops.

Then suddenly, I am snapped out of my thoughts by a gigantic tidal wave of accumulated dirty road water covering me and the bike as a car overtakes us. It stops me in my tracks – I can't believe what has just happened. As the cold water trickles down my neck, every inch of me now completely drenched, I wonder if the car might at least stop to apologise or to check that I hadn't in fact drowned. I mutter a few angry curse words under my breath and optimistically think, 'Well, at least now it can't get any worse.'

A few minutes later it happens again. I go to mutter some more angry curse words but instead I just whimper, being too tired to actually cry. Head down, there is nothing for it but to continue.

Ten minutes later, it happens again. Then immediately after that it happens a fourth time. Each time, a colossal wall of water rises from the semi-flooded roads and crashes over me from the side and above. I'm fairly certain that all four vehicles, but the last two motorhomes especially, have actually gone out of their way to create the surf – there was plenty of room to overtake and at the very least, they could have gone by slowly and thus reduced the wake they'd created. I picture them as smug and obnoxious tourists, laughing and congratulating each other at their hilarious practical joke at my expense.

So I snap at the last one. I scream obscenities into the air at full volume; I take a half-eaten energy bar out of its wrapper and throw it at them, challenging them to get out of the car and to not be so cowardly. I am a fiery ball of rage and I demand justice. Of course, ultimately I just feel like an ant throwing a crumb at an elephant – they just drive on, oblivious. Their tail lights disappear into the distance, leaving me once more alone, slowly pushing the bike up a hill that seems to be endless.

Desperately needing to dry out and warm up, I book into a hotel in Lochinver for the night. The only one available at such short notice happens to be a luxury resort. I arrive at a little past 7pm, rolling my grit covered bike into the softly lit reception room, soothing classical music playing gently in the background. I am leaving a small puddle of water wherever I go, to looks of both horror and bemusement from the fellow guests. But the receptionist cheerfully welcomes me, shows me the drying room where I can leave my bike and, as if she can read my mind, immediately reassures me that there is both a hot chocolate sachet and a kettle in my room.

Having checked in, I order room service and then devour my complimentary packet of shortbread biscuits whilst soaking in the bathtub, waiting for the feeling to return to my fingers and toes. I feel like both a total gangster and a complete wretch: utterly broken but also deeply satisfied at having emptied my energy bank so completely. It's a peaceful feeling to know you've given your all, you've won and you have no more to do. At least not until morning. After inhaling my dinner, I take some ibuprofen for the pain in my left leg, hoping it will also decrease the swelling, and I collapse into the magnificent bed, falling asleep instantly.

The next morning, I am unable to put much weight on my left leg without slightly wincing. All the same, I am sure it will loosen up, and I reason that I don't need to walk, I need to cycle, so it will be fine. Now at the halfway point, I sternly remind myself that failure is not an option. Reluctantly leaving the luxury hotel behind, I hit the road – thankful that it is at least a dry day.

My left leg continues to scream at me so I take some more ibuprofen and expect it to settle down. It takes me twice as long as usual to cover a mere eight kilometres, no doubt partly because I've been trying to cycle entirely with my right leg – I'm now unable to put any weight on my left leg without crying out in pain. With another 60 miles ahead of me as a minimum, I have to consider that I'm not going to hit my mileage today. I know that this means I won't be completing the challenge in time.

I've never been injured before, and my mind frantically rages with objections as I struggle to accept the facts. I wonder if I just need to push through the pain barrier, like I've done so many times before. There is little abuse my body won't tolerate – I've come to expect it to be unbreakable. Deep down, however, I know this is different. Tears have been rolling down my cheeks since leaving Lochinver, each pedal stroke is causing agony to shoot through my left leg. I accept the inevitable fact that I will go no further today. If I can rest it for a day and put some ice on it, maybe get a massage, I can fix it, I think.

It's a slow and painful return to Lochinver. I book into another hotel and ring friends to see if anyone can spare a few days to act as a support car, taking the weight off the bike so I can limp through to the finish on an unloaded bike. It's not how I wanted this journey to go but the thought of not finishing once again fills me with panic and clouds my judgement. I choose to ignore that I am now hobbling, totally unable to put weight on my left leg – I am desperate to finish by any means possible.

I manage to book a massage. I am greeted with a huge hug and, soon after, the warm hearted masseuse gently tells me the extent of the injury and that, although she knows this isn't what I want to hear, I will need to rest. Instinctively I know she is right.

Over the next day, it becomes clear that this isn't going to be a quick fix. My left quad is severely inflamed, with the right side of my body mal-adjusting to compensate. I limp around Lochinver, still quietly saying to myself that I'd be fine after a little rest. Alas, some things aren't fixed so quickly. After wrestling with it for the best part of two days, I finally accept this attempt of the North Coast 500 is over. Continuing on, even if I could somehow ignore the pain, would mean risking long-term damage and even with all of my stubbornness, I can't justify it.

For the second time in my relatively short adventure career, I am faced with failure. For the second time, I have given 110 per cent and it just hasn't been enough to get to the finish line. For hours, I beat myself up and consider all the people I think I have let down. I think of every critic, real and imagined, who will cheer at the news. With a heavy heart, I make the announcement, feeling very sorry for myself as I type the words 'Sorry, guys – I didn't go down without a fight'. I then go on to make the arrangements to somehow get back to Inverness.

To do this I arrange to first spend a night with my friend Will Copestake and family, in nearby Ullapool. I'll then be getting the bus from Ullapool back to Inverness the next afternoon and from there getting the sleeper train back to London that night. I arrive at the Copestakes' with a heavy heart and I'm forever grateful that after a warm welcome and 24 hours of near-constant laughter I left it feeling much lighter.

Will, a fellow adventurer, is no stranger to curveballs either. He tells me that he'd had to pull out of a challenge last year, also due to injury. As we share a hearty meal around the dinner table, his family offer me their sympathy but also their reassurance that a temporary disappointment is just that – temporary, not something that defines you. More stories of mishaps and adventures pepper the evening.

As I settle down to sleep in the spare room that night, my own critical voices are a little quieter, too. Preparing for a backlash like I'd experienced a couple of years ago, I brace myself as I check social media for the response to my announcement that I've had to pull out of my challenge. I'd been imagining the vitriolic headlines since making the announcement: 'Pathetic Adventurer Fails Again – Why Doesn't She Just Stop Embarrassing Herself?' So I am humbled to discover that not one person has berated me, or seems to think less of me, or indeed has a single bad word to say about the challenge not working out. Instead, I am greeted by hundreds of messages of heartfelt support.

Will further helps snap me out of my sulk by taking me kayaking in the glorious loch behind the house. My left leg may not have been functioning properly but both arms are fine, so he bundles me up in his spare kayaking gear and I marvel at Scotland's beauty from a whole different angle.

I leave the Copestakes feeling so much lighter than when I'd arrived. For the first time in years, I started to make peace with failure. As the coach rolls back through the mountains towards Inverness, I decide that I couldn't change what had happened in Russia any more than I could heal my torn quad overnight – it's time to stop trying to outrun failure, to let it go and trust that adversity has genuinely made me stronger. After all, that's why I'd started endurance adventures in the first place. I'd felt like I was wasting my potential, I'd wanted a chance to grow and over-come challenges. It seemed ridiculous in hindsight that I thought I could control what sort of challenges were reasonable.

For two years, I'd been desperately trying to outrun failure and control every narrative detail of my life. Eight kilometres outside of Lochinver in the Scottish Highlands, failure had chased me down and pinned me into submis-sion. I realised now that if I really am going to live a life of exploration and if I am committed to pushing myself out of my comfort zone then I will need to accept that failure is sometimes – perhaps often – going to be a real possibility. Does that mean that I should only take on projects where I knew I could succeed? Does that mean that I'd rather have an untarnished track record than grow as a person and actually find out what I might be capable of? Somewhere deep inside of me, that same spark of courage that had inspired me to take on the Volga against all odds shouted out in defiance. A life without risk was a life without colour: I'm not here to play it safe.

THE NEXT FEW months were spent patiently waiting for my leg to heal. This necessary stillness slowed me down and forced me to look inward. Rather than trying to exorcise (/exercise) my gremlins, I sat down with them over a cup of tea and told them that they'd had a pretty good run, but I was taking back the steering wheel now. I knew they'd never leave completely but I was done with letting them direct my actions. It was time to own the failures that had formed such an important part of my story, to accept my flaws that made me human and celebrate all that I'd achieved so far.

Instead of trying to brush failure under the carpet, I openly embraced it and spent months publicly talking about the importance of failure. What had once felt like a dirty little secret was now out in the open and an important section of my talks – I finally refused to be ashamed about it. I realised that every person that had ever inspired me had embraced their setbacks and it was time for me to do the same.

My last talk of the year took place at my friend Dave Cornthwaite's festival, Yestival. Now in its third year, this would be my third time speaking at the event and I decided to try something a little different. In front of hundreds of people, I began telling my story of how I came to make a career out of endurance challenges – all the usual anecdotes of leaving behind the job I hated, that initial leap of faith in California and the character building adventures that had followed since. This time, however, I guided my talk towards the uncomfortable topic of failure and lingered there – talking about all the failures I'd experienced and how the mental repercussions and stigma of failure often far outweigh any physical effects of endurance challenges. I embraced my feeling of vulnerability and confessed to my assembled audience that I'd frequently battled with an inner gremlin over the years who loved to berate my every mistake and constantly tell me how I wasn't good enough, strong enough or brave enough. I knew I wasn't alone – research shows that the average person talks to him/herself approximately 50,000 times a day, with most of that talk being about yourself. Furthermore, according to psychological research, a whopping 80 per cent (!) of that self-talk is negative. With each and every thought affecting every cell in our bodies and ultimately dictating the lives we lead, what is the answer?

You can only reason with a gremlin up to a point, I suggested. Eventually, you have to get physical. Ever since I could remember, I have danced to make myself better. Not the subtle or gentle dancing you do in polite company – the totally unreserved, carefree and no holds barred type of dancing that leaves you drenched in sweat and breathless – the sort you do when no one is watching. Because, it's a little known fact, but I'm sure that gremlins have no rhythm and they hate dancing.

That night, after one of the toughest years I'd ever known – a year that had brought me to my knees several times, both physically and emotionally – I stood on that stage in a Surrey field and I claimed back my space. I took a deep breath and led a packed tent in violently shaking off – quite literally – their gremlins and self-doubt as the song 'Happiest Man Alive' by Michael Montano blasted out. Seconds before I'd cued the music, my stomach had jumped into my throat. I hadn't told Dave what I had planned and I had no idea how people were going to react. I wondered if I was about to be left enthusiastically wiggling around on stage by myself in front of a crowd of unimpressed strangers who would all think I was a bit deranged. I needn't have worried – immediately, the audience began to move. The harder I danced, the harder they danced. I looked out to a sea of smiling people waving their arms and legs around, jumping up and down. Bodies everywhere pulsed and gyrated to the music like they'd all been possessed by the spirit of Beyoncé – the energy in that marquee was electric. It was rowdy and it was glorious. The minute we stopped dancing, the crowd happily roared and cheered – I guess we'd all really needed to blow off some steam.

That night, I peacefully curled up in my tent and thought of the unsure woman that had nervously first spoken at the first Yestival three years before, soon after returning from Ireland, and the bold and confident woman I had become. Much like we often reflect on our lives during birthdays, as I happily drifted off to sleep, I thought of how, in the 12 months since speaking at the previous year's festival, I'd been through hell and it felt like I'd finally come back up for fresh air. I'd survived, I hadn't been beaten and, stronger for overcoming the struggle, I knew my days of playing small were over.

If endurance challenges have taught me anything, it's that suffering can be a great teaching tool. Every tough experience I've had – from heartbreak to self-inflicted adventure-based misery to scraping by on multiple jobs and living off baked beans – has made me stronger. My resilience has been forged in tears and sweat. In hindsight, even the seemingly most sinister and cruel of life's plot twists have turned out to be a blessing in disguise when I've looked back on them later. Maybe you're not comfortable with having this kind of faith in how the universe works. That's obviously fine, too. Regardless, I've found one of the best attitudes to take in times of trouble can be summed up with a simple, but powerful question: what can I learn from this? If you ask better questions from life, you get better answers.

Over the rest of that festival weekend, people repeatedly came up to me to say how reassuring they found it to know that they weren't the only ones weighed down by self-doubt, and also to tell me how much they'd absolutely loved dancing it out. I went on to build more events around mental resilience and the importance of unleashing your inner (sometimes dancing) warrior. It always fills my heart with pure joy when I then get messages from people who have attended those events, and who have since taken to dancing around their various kitchens, bedrooms and office boardrooms. Next time you feel deflated, I invite you to join us – turn the volume up, go all in and sweat it out.

Don't let the gremlin drive; it will never lead you to anywhere worth going.

7 ALL THE GODDAMN WAY

'Go all the way with it. Do not back off. For once, go all the
goddamn way with what matters'
— Ernest Hemingway

I began 2018 with a series of talks and filming projects
that were all very exciting in their own right, but
above everything else, I knew that this was the year I
wanted to pull off my biggest adventure yet. It felt risky and
almost counterintuitive to take time out from it all — I had
lots of requests to do talks coming in and brand collabora-
tion offers now landing in my inbox on a weekly basis. I
seemed to be doing pretty well and didn't really have
anything to prove to anyone. Except I did — to myself. I
wanted to take on a challenge so huge that I knew I might
fail — physically, mentally, emotionally. I wanted to go all in.
I wanted to prove to myself that I could still go all in.

The adventure idea itself came easy enough; the
courage to follow through took a little bit longer.

The North Sea Cycle Route – otherwise known as Eurovelo 12 – is the world's longest signposted cycle route and it covers 3,700 miles and eight countries. Starting out in Scotland, it heads down through England and then over to France, progressing onwards through Belgium, the Netherlands, Germany, Denmark and Sweden, before eventually finishing in Norway.

As a I started to research the route, waves of unadulterated excitement rippled through my veins – all those countries, all those sights! This was huge – a challenge I could really sink my teeth into again. It was time. Or was it? Inevitably, my gremlin soon piped up with all the reasons this was a totally terrible idea and why I should set my sights on something smaller. I tried to appease the gremlin by making a pros and cons list, tackling self-doubt with logic. First off all the reasons NOT to go – this bit was easy:

Money: Shouldn't I be spending my money more responsibly? How about finally saving for that mortgage and IKEA furniture?

Time: It was going to be huge chunk out of my year – saying yes to this would inevitably mean saying no to other opportunities. Talks, brands partnerships, etc were going so well – was it wise to take three months off in the middle of it all? I knew I'd also miss countless celebrations with family and friends – my birthday included, but also the birth of my nephew. That last one stung a bit.

Fitness: 3,700 miles is a long way, could my legs do it? Would I get injured again?

Mechanics: With the exception of knowing a few basics, I didn't know how to fix a bike. Every year I'd meant to do a basic bike mechanics course but had never gotten round to it. Would I end up stranded in the middle of nowhere with a problem I couldn't fix?

Failure: The favourite excuse of my inner gremlin, who liked to bash this particular concern over my head on a regular basis. Wouldn't it be SO embarrassing to fail again? Jeez, LK – you'd never live it down!

And then it was time to balance this list out with all the reasons that I SHOULD go. I stared blankly at that side of the page, searching within my soul for all the reasons this trip was a brilliant idea. Eventually, this is what I came up with:

I like riding my bike.

I have never been to Norway.

It was the final country that sealed the deal for me – I'd always wanted to go to Norway and couldn't think of a better way to get there. The comparison list got thrown out – since when was adventure logical anyway? There would always be more reasons to take the safe option, but that's no way to live. So what if I failed? I didn't want to be looking back on my life as a wrinkled old lady, regretting the things I wasn't brave enough to at least try. My stomach flipped with a mix of absolute terror and complete excitement – I knew this was the one. The Great North Ride was born.

First things first, Scotland and I had some unfinished business. Completing the loop of the North Coast 500 seemed like ideal training for the two and a half months that were to follow. And so April came around and once more I found myself on a sleeper train headed to Inverness. Struggling to sleep again because unlike last time I knew exactly what I was in for – those fierce hills were not to be underestimated. But also unlike last time, this time, I was ready for a fight.

Unfortunately, Scotland was also ready for a fight. Arriving into Inverness, I was greeted by bright blue skies and glorious sunshine, which lulled me into a false sense of security. A punishing and unyielding headwind loyally stuck with me all day. My legs and lungs burnt as I battled away, only to achieve a lamentable average speed of 10mph. I was relieved when the day ended. So much for easing myself into things gently, I thought, shortly before collapsing into a deep sleep.

The next morning, I was once more greeted by bright skies and sunshine. I refused to check the wind forecast for the day and instead braced myself for the worst. I blasted out some power tunes as I spooned mouthfuls of porridge and peanut butter into my mouth – psyching myself up for battle.

Scotland would be sneaky today though. For a couple of absolutely blissful hours, the fierce wind lovingly nudged me along in the right direction, pushing my average speed up to an exhilarating 19mph – no mean feat on a fully loaded bike. Just when this had persuaded me that I was in for a relatively easy day, I turned into the wind and was promptly slowed back down to a soul destroying 5mph. All day, the wind toyed with my emotions. One moment my biggest cheerleader and ally, the next my arch nemesis. Ultimately, I had to conclude it was being harsh but fair.

Later on I passed a fellow cyclist, who was going in the opposite direction to me. He made sure to cheerfully let me know that further up the road was a stag really close to the road, apparently quite tame. I thanked the cyclist but I thought I'd probably just check the stag out in passing and not stop. As a general rule, I try to keep stopping times to an absolute minimum during challenges. I find that if I stop for too long, I lose all motivation to get going again. I still had 30 miles to go and, as always, I was keen to get the mileage completed as soon as I could so I could maximise my rest time.

Well, that was the plan until I turned the corner and saw him – a young male stag, standing majestically in the heather, a few cars parked nearby and their passengers standing in awe. He was absolutely beautiful and completely mesmerizing. I slowly pedalled over, placing my bike gently down on the nearby gravel before cautiously walking over. He didn't flinch. I gently edged a little closer. He calmly met my gaze and there we stood for a few minutes. He seemed so peaceful and completely unfazed by his small but magnetised audience. I imagined all the wisdom this magnificent creature could be trying to express to us all, perhaps some impactful and significant words on the power of nature and the deep connection so vital for all of us, that so many of us have lost touch with as we get tangled up in the noise of modern life. I imagined how he'd be telling us to value our time above all and to protect the planet, to value its resources more than we value the pointless consumerism proliferated by marketing. In reality, I expect he was a little disappointed that I didn't have any food for him and he soon resumed grazing.

I pedalled onwards and upwards, smiling to myself for the rest of the afternoon. I switched my music off for the rest of the day and just drank in the scenery: the rolling mountains, the seemingly unending roads and, eventually, the sparkling aquamarine water alongside the coast where I finished the day. Scotland can be cruel, but every now and then it offers a glimpse of magic which makes it utterly unforgettable.

The next morning, however, the gloves came off. Getting ready to retrace the section I'd injured my leg on last year, I knew I was in for a tough day of unrelenting climbs. I began nervously and eventually settled into a rhythm. That was until the headwind returned and picked a fight for no reason I could determine. It slowed me down to a devastating 4mph for the whole day. It never ceased and I had to fight for every mile. With 20 miles left to go, I had a complete sense of humour failure and I took the wind situation very personally; I had thought that Scotland and I might be becoming friends but clearly I was wrong.

Ten excruciatingly slow miles later, I decided to fight back and snap myself out of my pointless bad mood. I deployed the emergency bar of mint chocolate Aero and sang Led Zeppelin at full volume into the wind. Doing my best Mel Gibson in *Braveheart* impression, I also manically screamed: 'You can take my average speed, Scotland, but you cannot take my freedom to siiiiiiing.' A notable side effect of spending so much time by myself is apparently my willingness to chat away to places, animals and weather conditions alike. The power combo of chocolate and bike-karaoke worked brilliantly, as it nearly always does, and I finished the day shattered, but happy.

Made wary by last year's injury, I'd broken this section into two pieces so the following day was to be a brilliantly short 30 miles, intended as an active rest day of sorts to look after my leg, as I was still unsure how it would cope. 'It's only 30 miles, how bad can it be?' I thought, apparently forgetting where I was.

The first section of the day was full of breathtaking views. I found myself on a magical single-track road, lochs to my left and mountain views stretching out in front of me as far as I could see. As sunlight dappled on the water below, I found my average speed slowing down again – for once, not because of the terrain or headwind, but because I was in no hurry to speed through the captivating scenery. This wasn't so bad, was it?

However, as I neared the end of the section, I instantly

understood how I'd injured my leg last year – up, up, up I climbed, my legs screaming at me. Even with the lower mileage target, this day was packing a hefty punch with well over 1,000 metres of elevation to cover. It was as if Scotland had sensed me falter and, like the predator it was, seized the chance to really strike when it would hurt most. Torrential rain showers pummelled down, channels of water rushing along the roads. In an attempt to keep my spirits up, I began to narrate the situation out loud in various, terribly cliched accents.

'Cor blimey, Guvnaaa! It's 'ammering it daaaan,' said the cockney

'I know, right? Such a bummer. Like, surf's up, dude! Except there's no surf . . . ' said the bohemian Californian.

'To be sure, to be sure. I could do with a noice cup o'tea,' agreed the Irish.

'Oooh aye. It's a wee bit nippy here noo,' sympathised the Scottish.

I rolled into Lochinver, once more resembling a drowned rat. I wondered if I'd ever arrive in Lochinver any other way, and considered that perhaps this was just part of the mandatory toll you had to pay to reach somewhere so beautiful. I imagined a Scottish version of Gandalf the Wizard from *Lord of the Rings* awaiting cyclists on the outskirts, yelling 'YOU SHALL NOT PASS', whilst holding a garden hose ready to soak those who insisted they continue.

Completely drenched, I treated myself to a B&B. Owner Colin warmly welcomed me into his home and kindly hung up my soaking wet clothes in the conservatory. I sat in my beautiful, cosy room cooking a dinner of instant noodles with lumps of Babybel cheese thrown in on my camping stove by the window, hoping the distinct scent of 'chicken' noodles wasn't pervading through to the other immaculately decorated rooms. Anxiously, I contemplated the next day. Tomorrow would be the moment of truth. Lochinver had reminded me of the song 'Hotel California' by the Eagles – 'You can check out anytime you like, but you can never leave'. As beautiful as this town was, I really hoped I'd finally be leaving it behind tomorrow.

The next morning, I devoured a hearty breakfast of scrambled eggs with toast, pancakes (Colin insisted he was making them anyway so I really should have some – who was I to argue) and Weetabix with bananas. Part comfort eating, part fuelling strategy; I remembered all too well that the first thing that awaited me was a steady climb out of Lochinver and I hoped that the extra food would give me the strength I needed. This was it.

Up I climbed, half-expecting my leg to scream in protest again, anxiously waiting for the moment I'd have to face defeat once more . . . But the breaking point never came. My legs burned, they ached and they struggled – but they loyally (albeit reluctantly) obeyed my demands. Slowly but stubbornly, we pushed on. After an hour, I realised I'd passed the point of last year's injury.

'WAAAAAAAAAAHOOOOOOOOOO' I screamed at full volume into the wilderness. There was no one around to hear it but I added an unbridled 'YEAAAAAAAAAAAAAAHHHHHHH' shortly after. Then, more quietly, I softly added, 'Thank you, legs. I knew you had it in you.'

I decided a celebratory shortbread biscuit was in order, followed by a celebratory wee behind a bush – then I promptly pedalled on. After all, I still had the other half of this route to complete so the challenge wasn't over yet. I had no idea what lay around the corner now and I was excited to find out.

Naturally, what lay around the corner was hills, headwind and more hills. But I repeatedly thought back to the me of last year that who didn't get to climb any of these hills. I thought about how I'd literally limped home, defeated, weary, grieving and frustrated. How very happy I felt now to be able to sweat and struggle my way up and over this unforgiving terrain. My wheels slid over winding roads with views over yet more stunning lochs and mountains and I mused over how grateful I was to be suffering, and wondered if that was perhaps a little bit weird. As the skies cleared and the sunshine dappled on the water, I was speechless. After four days of throwing everything at me, it was as if Scotland was rewarding me for passing a test. For the rest of the afternoon I didn't sing, or shout, or talk to myself. I just silently marvelled at the incredible, awe-inspiring landscape I was riding through.

A friend of mine, Raphael Rychetsky, happened to also be in Scotland with his motorbike and halfway up a hill, he tracked me down.

'It's YOU,' said Raphael merrily, his voice muffled by his helmet.

'Yep!' I panted, in between very heavy breathing. 'It's me . . .' I replied, adding absolutely nothing of value to this friendly exchange. Truthfully, I'd completely forgotten that Raphael was in Scotland, so when he cheerfully pulled up next to me to say hello, as I was dripping in sweat and panting my way up yet another seemingly endless climb, all I could think was, 'Who is this strange bloke and why doesn't he realise that I'm not in the mood for a little chat right now?'

Raphael, sensing my lack of enthusiasm for conversation, motioned that he would wait for me at the top of the hill. As soon as he sped off into the distance and I cursed Dory for her lack of engine, I realised who it was and felt incredibly guilty for being so abrupt, especially considering we'd been coordinating for days about meeting up and Raphael had been regularly checking if I wanted him to bring me any supplies. Raphael is a very talented photographer and had also generously offered to take some photos, so my second thought upon realising who it was, was 'Please don't let me have to get off and push my bike up this monster of a hill.' Sweat dripped into my eyes and my legs howled with the build up of lactic acid, but I was determined to save face and conquer this climb. Eventually I reached the top where Raphael was waiting – his smile beaming. Immediately, we exchanged a huge, sweaty hug.

'I'm SO sorry! I didn't realise it was you, I just thought there was this weird bloke chatting to me and I was like "Dude, clearly not a good time?!" I'm so happy to see you!' I laughed.

Not even the slightest bit offended, Raphael offered me some chocolate and we caught up on the last few days. Wary of the fact that I still had 20 miles to cover, which would of course take me a lot longer than him, we made a plan to meet up in Durness later that day. Raphael sped off into the distance – soon he was a speck on the horizon and then I was alone once more.

Whatever envy I'd felt for Raphael's speed vanished for the final section. I found myself on a long, largely flat and winding single track road surrounded by mountains. It was extraordinary. I pitied anyone who rushed through terrain like this.

Rolling wearily into Durness at 6pm, having climbed a total of 1,400 metres throughout the day, I pulled straight to the local shop with one thing on my mind: Orange Fanta. Coming out of the shop I spotted Raphael, chatting away to a group of seven burly motorcyclists.

'Yeah, we hit the road at 9am this morning. That final section was pretty tough,' said one.

'Mmm. That wind,' agreed another.

Smiling to myself, thinking definitions of 'tough sections' were definitely relative, I made my way over to say hello, my cleats clicking on the ground, and both Dory and I feeling very small in comparison to these large men and their powerful bikes. Raphael introduced me, I in turn introduced Dory and we all exchanged route notes from the day. Somewhat in disbelief that anyone would be attempting this route on a loaded bike without an engine, they offered me various snacks, seeming very concerned that I was 'only a little thing' and would need all the energy I could get. It didn't seem polite to argue – sticks of cheese, nuts, an apple and of course more chocolate were all gladly consumed in between delicious gulps of Orange Fanta. Although we clearly differed in our preferred means of travel, we all agreed that the single-track road leading into Durness had to be one of the most stunning roads any of us had ever seen and that Scotland's rugged beauty was hard to beat.

The group gradually dispersed, as they each had at least another 50 miles to ride before stopping for the day. I'd booked myself into a nearby B&B again and Raphael was camping so we made plans to meet up for dinner after getting sorted at our respective homes for the night. I was just dreaming about the hot shower that awaited me, when I realised that my B&B was situated on the top of a very large hill. My heart sank. If there's one thing I've learnt about Scotland, it's that it will always demand you climb one more hill than you feel capable of. That extra hill is always there, lurking around the corner, waiting to catch you out when you least expect it. Expressed as a mathematical equation: $n+1$.

I made it, and was warmly welcomed into the home of Tony and Jill. It turned out they were keen mountain runners who organised ultra races nearby, and so no words of explanation were needed as to why I'd decided to cycle through the Highlands. My energy dwindling, I grabbed a quick shower before meeting Raphael for dinner in the local hotel/restaurant/tourist information centre. I opted for pizza and, minutes after finishing it, realised I was barely able to keep my eyes open. Luckily for me, Raphael is not easily offended and completely understood that my bed was calling.

Groggily rubbing my eyes the next morning, I could hear the rain lashing down outside and the wind howling. Instinctively, I hugged the duvet closer and groaned to myself. I couldn't think of a single good reason to get out of bed, and I lay staring up at the ceiling, desperately trying to will myself into action. It is only when the smell of fresh coffee filtered into my room that I remembered that I had a hearty breakfast to look forward to. Food, glorious food – the best motivator there is for a weary cyclist. Slowly, I got to my feet, my legs stiff and aching, and I hobbled around the room, reluctantly packing up my panniers.

In between the multiple rounds of food that Jill brings to the breakfast table, she cheerfully reassures me that I have some beautiful views to look forward to. Looking out of the window art the grey, blustery landscape, I am not so sure that I believe her, but by the time I've finished a cafetière of fresh coffee, I feel ready either way. Keen to take full advantage of the coffee buzz before it wears off, I hit the road at just past 8am, pleasantly surprised to discover that it had stopped raining.

After an hour on the road, I am beginning to optimistically consider that perhaps the weather forecast had been wrong for today and maybe there wouldn't be any more rain after all. Jill had been right, too – this section is stunning. Alas, no sooner had I stopped to appreciate the view than the heavens opened. I hastily changed into my waterproofs and heavy winter gloves as the rain lashed down. It just so happened that today was also going to be the longest mileage of the whole trip – I was in for a long, soggy day.

The thick gloves made it tricky to open anything on the move so I wasn't eating; I'd also become obsessed with not stopping, even to pee. I wanted to get this section over and done with as quickly as possible. Alas, with 1,700 metres of elevation and 70 miles to cover on a bike weighed down by panniers, speed was a relative term. All day, I kept hitting a wall and considered that if zombies could learn to ride a bike, they'd probably be doing it in a more impressive fashion than I was. The rain continued to hammer down at me, and it was all I could do to gradually edge my way forwards. I tortured myself with thoughts of being back home and cosily tucked up on the sofa with a blanket, a cup of tea and a good adventure book. What I wouldn't give to be warm, dry and reading about someone else's 'character building' misery right now.

By lunchtime, I realised that my 'speed' tactic was totally futile and that I should know better; when you're burning thousands of calories each day it's essential to eat and drink regularly. I'd just have to accept that this would take as long as it was going to take. I was well and truly in my pain cave now and I just had to embrace that I wouldn't be out of it anytime soon. Unsurprisingly, making the effort to both regularly eat and hydrate did wonders for both energy levels and morale.

All day the rain hammered down, all day the wind whipped around, chilling my exposed face as I defiantly edged towards Thurso. I'd again booked myself into a local hotel so I could dry my clothes, and get a proper meal and a hot shower. Such simple things, but those thoughts had been my beacon of hope all day. It felt like the rain had not only soaked through my waterproofs but also like the cold had actually permeated my bones. Scotland hadn't beaten me yet but I was paying a price for it – I was wrecked. At that moment, I wanted absolutely nothing more from my life than to be warm.

I checked into the hotel and, once again, I found myself unable to prioritise between food and a hot shower, so I ended up doing both – eating a CLIF energy bar in the shower as a pre-dinner snack, whilst willing my core temperature to rise. Dinner that night was once again a packet of instant noodles cooked on my camping stove, with a tin of mackerel and some crackers crumbled over the top for 'texture' and a couple of small packets of butter added in for extra fat. I'd learnt in Ireland to add butter to everything as a useful way of boosting calories. As always, I was struggling to eat enough and this made it simpler. Immediately after dinner, I wearily clambered into bed, falling asleep to the sound of my clothes drip-dripping on to the bathroom tiles nearby. I'd put all of the radiators on as high as they would go and I hoped that both my clothes and I would thaw out overnight.

The next morning, protectively hugging my duvet around me, I tentatively opened the curtains, desperately hoping that it wouldn't be raining, as the thought of spending another day under constant showers filled me with absolute dread. There were bright blue skies once more! I checked the weather forecast to make sure Scotland wasn't pulling one of its cruel tricks and was delighted to see that it did indeed look dry all day. In my excitement, I forgot to check the wind direction, which was probably for the best.

After filling up on another hearty Scottish breakfast, I hit the road at 9am. Immediately, any thoughts of optimism I'd had vanished. A strong gust of wind violently slapped me in the face, setting the tone for the rest of the day. I quickly put all of my waterproof outer layers back on, hoping they might act as a windbreaker. It seemed cruel and disorientating to have such beautifully sunny skies and such brutally cold winds. I silently pleaded with Scotland: 'Please, send more rain if you must – lashings of it! Anything but a headwind this strong.' Naturally, this had absolutely no effect on the weather conditions and all day I battled against the wind.

I tried all of my regular mood-boosting tricks – singing, chocolate, scenery appreciation – none of it worked. I couldn't bring myself to smile at all. As a coping strategy, I decided to personify the headwind, naming her Helga. In lieu of being able to cheer myself up, I decided I was going to war with Helga instead. Helga became the sole focus of all of my frustrations; I imagined her taunting me, willing me to quit.

Helga never let up and all day it was a ceaseless struggle to keep moving forward. Sometimes, a particularly strong gust would stop me in my tracks and, at other moments, I'd get blown across the road – particularly terrifying when there were lorries nearby. It was one of the only times I was grateful for the extra weight on the bike. Mostly, Helga consistently charged directly at me, forcing me to fight hard for each and every mile.

Wearily arriving into Golspie, I all but staggered into the local shop, half crazed with exhaustion. A ball of mozzarella, a pack of smoked salmon, pasta parcels filled with spinach and cheese, a 'family sized' bar of chocolate, shortbread biscuits, a caramel milkshake, crisps – it all went into the shopping basket, and that night I threw an eclectic food party for one and crammed food in like a woman possessed until I was about to burst. I happily passed out moments later.

'I wonder what weather Scotland will throw at me today?' I thought, as I began the final day. Whatever it was, I was determined to face it with a smile after having spent the last couple of days feeling miserable. After all, today was a day of celebration – it was the final day!

Always eager to keep me on my toes, Scotland apparently decided that the final day was going to be a remix of its greatest weather hits. I was treated to the mega mash up – clear blue skies, rain storms, ferocious winds, blazing hot sunshine. In fact, that final day had almost every kind of weather condition possible, apart from the one I so desperately wished for – a tailwind. It seemed that no matter what direction the wind blew in, it was never behind me. At times, it really felt like Scotland was going out of its way to tease and provoke me. I decided that the best revenge for this cruel behaviour was to not let it bother me at all. That would surely take all the fun out of it for Scotland and ruin its spiteful game completely. On the final day, I gritted my teeth and forced myself to be absurdly positive about everything: 'Oh, Helga is back! Excellent news! This will be making my legs stronger for Norway – thanks, Helga!'

'Ah, a sudden rain shower! Brilliant. I'd have obviously

been devastated to bring my waterproofs and not need them – what a waste of weight and space that would have been!'

'A gigantic hill with 14 per cent incline and a 23mph headwind? JACKPOT!'

In all honesty, I managed this positive outlook to varying degrees of success throughout the day, but it was definitely better than sulking. I tried to savour the views, feeling both ready to finish and a little sad to be leaving the magic of the Scottish Highlands behind. I tried to dismiss the fact that I felt destroyed – after all, this was merely the warm up lap to a much bigger challenge. But in truth, the thought of the Great North Ride now filled me with panic. This week had been, at times, absolute hell. How on earth was I going to manage over two months?! I pushed the thought out of my mind and continued on to Inverness. The Great North Ride was three weeks away – first things first, it was time to finish this.

Arriving back into Inverness, I thought of all that had happened in the eight days since I'd left it and all that had happened in the months since my first visit. I welled up as I cycled over the Kessock bridge as it finally dawned on me that I wasn't going to fail again, that I'd actually made it! It had felt like such a risk attempting this again and I hadn't dared to consider it a success until there was absolutely no way I could fail. That moment was now, I think I could well have been the happiest person in Inverness.

'Hey bridge, how you doin'?' I hollered, in my best Joey from *Friends* impression. 'INVERNESS BABY!' I screamed soon after.

Raphael was waiting in Velocity, a nearby cycling café. I'd been told about this café a few times – renowned as much for its delicious cake as much as its friendly staff. I hadn't made it here last time as I'd wanted to save the celebratory slice of cake for my moment of triumph. Naturally, the café was on top of another large hill – n+1 in action once more. I sat in the café with Raphael for a couple of hours – warming my hands around a cup of tea, feeling a quiet sense of contentment. There had been so many low points over the past eight days – so many gut-wrenching, soul searching moments of suffering – but here I was, having completed my challenge, sitting in a café with a nice cup of tea. Nan would have loved this story, I thought. It may have taken me a bit longer than planned, but I'd made it.

I waved goodbye to Raphael and headed towards the train station to check into the sleeper train, with just enough time to get a takeaway pizza on the way. I leant Dory against a pole outside the station, the pizza box resting across the panniers, and I happily ate my pizza as the people of Inverness rushed around me. I remembered how it felt to be at this very same station last year – I'd felt cheated and bitterly disappointed, tears rolling down my cheeks as I limped onto the train. As with most tough moments, if only we knew what was around the corner I'm sure we wouldn't cry so much.

In hindsight, the misadventure of last year had finally given me some sense of peace around the idea of failure. It had taught me perspective, and patience, and perhaps most importantly, it had taught me to face down some of my harshest critics, notably the ones that reside in my own head. I still wouldn't ever be accepting failure without a fight, but it had made it OK should I ever do my best, and that not quite be enough. This victory was infinitely more rewarding because of the failure that came before it. I finished my pizza, slowly wandered over to the train and I'd fallen asleep with a gentle smile on my face before the train had pulled out from the station.

BACK HOME, I had just under three weeks until I would be packing up Dory for the Great North Ride. Although I'd decided on the date some time ago, it suddenly felt way too soon. Adventures always have this nasty habit of sneaking up on me. My body felt wrecked from eight days of Scottish hills and headwinds and the thought of gearing myself up to go all over again – for much, much longer – was overwhelming. I knew my legs needed to recover, but I also began panicking about my fitness levels. Should I rest or should I train? Ultimately, I knew my legs would adapt, but I was heading back to Scotland for the start of the ride and I was under no illusions that this would be a gentle warm up.

The panic spread, like a virus, to infect my packing process, too. I spent three days unpacking, repacking, swearing at panniers, ordering new panniers, going back to the old panniers . . . extra pants in, extra pants out, arguing back and forth with myself for hours on end. All the while, well-intentioned friends and relatives all seemed to be asking the same cheerful question: 'Are you excited?'

'Yes, can't wait!' I would enthusiastically reply, trying to hide the fact that I actually felt irritable, stressed and prone to tears.

Despite getting ready to head off on ta huge adventure, the type I'd always dreamt of, I felt a pang of sadness for all those special occasions I knew I'd miss. When I'm reminded that I'll be missing the birth of my nephew by a day, more tears ensue. The slightest thing was liable to cause me to feel hugely aggrieved, far beyond what was reasonable. I am normally so good at rolling with it and looking for the positive, rather than focusing on the negative, but I confess there was little perspective to be found in the days leading up to the Great North Ride.

It eventually dawned on me that the prickly mood was a poor attempt to cover up nerves – I was all twisted up in apprehension. At the heart of it, remained that fear I knew so well – I was worried I would fail and by failing embarrass myself, let down supporters and sponsors, doom my speaking career for all eternity, and bring great lingering shame to my family in the process. Logically, I was quite sure that no one else actually thought of it that way, but unfortunately, logic didn't really come into it. My inner gremlin was just running wild and I was less able to keep it in check than usual. And for good measure, I added a layer of guilt on top of all of that for not being more excited.

Mum, however, being hugely positive at all times, remained stubbornly optimistic throughout the packing/repacking process, despite her home once more being turned into Adventure Preparation HQ with her lounge floor perpetually covered in lycra, baby wipes and various piles of bike related paraphernalia.

'Oh, that looks the best it has done yet!'

'I'm sure this next trick [arbitrarily removing one small item and slightly rejigging the setup in a desperate attempt to defy the laws of physics] is the key to it.'

'FANTASTIC! Looks great!' (Even when the pannier is bursting at the seams and I can barely close it.)

Ever keen to help, Mum also frequently calls out impossibly impractical but very creative suggestions. Unfortunately, she frequently gets the names for things mixed up, which is both infuriating and endearing all at once: 'How about strapping the sleeping bag [tent] to the spokes [pannier rack]?'

As the stress builds, I default to no training because physical fitness seemed like the least of my worries. With lack of exercise, I feel lethargic and cranky – barely leaving my laptop as I finalise the many logistics and try to clear the backlog of admin that seems never-ending. I organise community rides in some of the places I'll be passing through, reach out to local schools and email back and forth with various PR agencies. I think about and plan blogs, content strategies, ferry timetables (there would be 27 ferries all together so this took a lot of coordination!), schedules.

The lesser known side of making a career from adventure is all of the work that accompanies it behind the scenes. Monetising my trips means, for example, that capturing decent images from the road is essential – for my own content, for the brands that are supporting me and for the stories I would be sharing, in print and through my talks, long after the adventure ended. It was no longer a case of pack up, get up and go – I was simultaneously my own press agent, speaking agent, community outreach officer, route planner and personal trainer. The same goes for most other adventurers I know – which is why I'm always inclined to respond to comments of, 'You're so lucky to do what you do' with a smile and a gentle reference to the well-known quote by a guy called Coleman Cox: 'I am a great believer in luck. The harder I work, the more of it I seem to have.'

I am, of course very lucky in many respects and I'm grateful for the opportunities available to me because of the relatively comfortable life I just happened to have been born into in the UK – but I work hard, too. I don't deny my advantages but it's also relevant to note the sacrifices I've made and the things I've prioritised in order to make this life possible. If anything, I think it's important to know how much is possible thanks to persistence, rather than dismiss other people's success as just 'luck'. Luck implies there's nothing you can do to influence the circumstance and, in my experience, this is rarely true.

Every night in the run up to departure, before I go to sleep, I find myself running through any number of (highly unlikely) unpleasant scenarios. I don't like to boast, but this is a game I often really excel at. For example, one night I imagine hundreds of angry wild rats appearing out of nowhere and surrounding my tent! How long would it take for them to chew through the tent fabric? How would you escape when totally outnumbered? How fast are rats? Would I be able to outrun them if I managed to shimmy out? Could I perhaps distract them with an edible decoy? Do rats like peanut butter?

My biggest fear is the bike breaking as it feels like I'm taking far too much stuff. I don't understand how I'd packed so light for Ireland a few years ago and I feel infuriated that apparently I've gotten worse instead of growing wiser over the years, despite my kit list being much more sophisticated. I had also meant to do an in-depth bike maintenance course by now but I haven't managed that. I'd picked up a few basics but, running out of time, I concluded that if something did go wrong and I couldn't fix the problem, I'd just have to find someone who could. Either way, worrying about it in advance wouldn't help.

Eventually, mostly because I got so fed up of repacking, I settled on a set up and decided that is it and I will just have to live with the consequences. Then, still feeling emotionally fragile from the whole process, I sneak some extra pants back in as a comfort.

The night before I'm due to set off, my pre-adventure brain unhelpfully doesn't let me sleep until midnight and then wakes me up four hours later, bombarding me with hundreds of 'Did you remember to pack the . . .?' and 'Don't forget to email . . .!' and 'What happens if the . . .breaks?' and 'OOH – Puffins! Maybe you'll see puffins!'

THE NEXT MORNING I wheel Dory out and together Mum and I roll to the local train station, much slower than usual due to the added weight of the panniers, where we say an emotional goodbye. I'm getting on a train for a seven-hour trip from London King Cross to Aberdeen first, then catching an overnight ferry from Aberdeen to Lerwick in the Shetland Islands. After the last couple of weeks' potent cocktail of nerves/excitement, it's a huge relief to at last be on my way.

As I settle into my seat on the train, I consider the mammoth journey I am about to start. I find myself deeply inhaling in an attempt to suppress the tears that are threatening to surface. I plug my earphones into my laptop, once more turning to the reliably calming sounds of Ludovico Einaudi's piano and focus on clearing the last bits of admin, all the while feeling totally overwhelmed. Luckily for me, I am not able to stew in my nerves for very long. Two elderly gentlemen soon join the train – Sandy sits to my right, next to the window, and Robbie sits opposite him. Old friends, they are cheerfully returning to Aberdeen from a weekend away.

It's a lovely summer's day and the views of the vast landscape that roll by our window become increasingly beautiful – clear blue skies and rich green fields stretch out in the distance, with the occasional tantalising glimpse of the very same sea I would soon be cycling alongside for the next couple of months. Over the next few hours, Sandy and Robbie keep me entertained with tales of local Scottish folklore and point out points of interest as we zoom by. They also keep me supplied with rhubarb and custard sweets, which we wash down with tea in between lots of laughter. They don't know that I boarded the train that morning feeling apprehensive and overwhelmed, but by the time we all arrived in Aberdeen, my pre-adventure brain had finally calmed down. I silently thank the adventure fairies for sending me Sandy and Robbie, and the simple acts of kindness that show up just when you need them.

8 YOU GET WHAT YOU GIVE

'CAN'T FORGET,

We only get what we give'
– 'You Get What You Give' by New Radicals

As the ferry pulls into Lerwick, I consider that I have a grand total of 3,700 miles ahead of me – a realisation that makes me not want to leave my cosy ferry cabin. I start the first day of the Great North Ride - the 14th May 2019 - with an empty tank courtesy of sea sickness on the ferry – intermittent sleep and an inability to eat more than a couple of mouthfuls came with the nausea as a package deal.

Thankfully I've arrived into Lerwick to both sunshine and a tailwind! This makes for a charmed first day and I instantly fall in love with Shetland. I also get over excited when I spot some Shetland ponies – the rather obvious fact that Shetland ponies comes from Shetland hadn't ever occurred to me before! My very delayed realisation makes me giggle every time I see them. The day is characterised by creamy smooth tarmac, smiling locals and dazzling scenery. Maybe I could just stay here . . .? I happily collapse into a hostel bed at the end of the day having successfully reached Skaw, the most northerly part of the UK and where the route will officially start, feeling absolutely exhausted but relieved to be making a start. At long last, the mileage count-down has begun.

The second day isn't so kind to me. Bright blue skies now combined with the return of Helga the headwind – yesterday's gentle breeze had turned into a 20+mph gusts hitting me head on. By the time I disembark from my second inter-island ferry of the day, I'm washed out and shivering – a situation not even fixed by a trusty can of Orange Fanta. Some kind souls on the ferry, seeing the state I'm in, gently suggest they give me a lift back into Lerwick. I'd planned to ride to Sunburgh (at the bottom of the island) and back the next day before getting an early evening ferry from Lerwick over to Orkney. Having already covered the equivalent distance, I grudgingly accept. The prospect of crawling forwards for a further four hours in this state didn't seem at all sensible. This is further highlighted when, in the car with my new friends and saviours, I notice I'm strug-gling to speak coherently. I try to point out a golf course that we're passing, only to discover that I apparently can't quite manage to say the word 'golf', instead muttering 'guh . . . guh' a couple of times before I decide just to be quiet.

Although I'm certainly not at my most eloquent, my inner gremlins are having no such problems and soon make their thoughts very clear: I am absolutely broken and it's only day two – how the hell do I think I'm going to survive the next couple of months? What an idiot. I can't do this. I'm not fit enough, and I'm not strong enough, and the bike seems to weigh at least as much as two large adult elephants.

I check into a local hotel in Lerwick in an attempt to recharge some more before getting yet another ferry – this time to Kirkwall – the next night. It would be my sixth ferry in five days and I'm already dreading the potential sea sickness that awaits. It all just seems a bit much.

That night, after drinking litres of water and eating the classic feast of yet more instant noodles with butter, I finally start to feel a bit better. As the encrusted sweat washes away in the hotel room shower, I feel a sharp sting on my left leg and arm as the water hits my skin – it's only then that I realise I'd gotten quite badly sunburnt. Suddenly, it all clicks into place and I realise why I'd been such a mess for most of the day – I'd been showing the early signs of heat exhaustion. I'd recently brushed up on some first aid skills with a medical friend, Steve Blethyn, and it all came flooding back. I'm relieved I hadn't let the gremlins win and carried on for another few hours, it would have undeniably made things a whole lot worse. As it is, I seem to have caught it just in time. I vow to be more careful and also to be more kind to myself going forwards. I have a long way to go and it's was absolutely pointless annihilating myself this early. Gremlins – o, LK – 1.

The next few days are gruelling. The bike feels offensively heavy; Helga the Headwind behaves completely obnoxiously and the inner gremlins are always lurking nearby. I realise that it's going to be a very long couple of months unless the gremlins and I come to some sort of agreement. I make a deal with them that they can only pipe up at the end of the day. Under no circumstances are they to voice their concerns during working hours, and any comments about the remaining mileage are particularly not at all welcome.

If ever I consider the sheer distance that I still have left to cover, I feel almost paralysed with despair. Usually the thought pops up as I'm lugging the bike up a long, arduous hill. The same concern, over and over: 'If you're struggling this much now, how are you going to achieve the rest?!' I do my very best to banish those kind of thoughts and, instead, I break down the day into smaller, manageable chunks – like getting to the next petrol station, where I could eat something that didn't involve peanut butter. These daily targets keep me sane. It would be impossible without them. I repeatedly lie to myself and pretend that all I have to do is get to that next arbitrary goal post – refusing to think of all the many, many goal posts still to come.

The section from John O'Groats to Tongue turns out to be the most sociable of the whole trip – I pass and frequently chat to dozens of cyclists. Most of them are headed in the opposite direction, nearing the end of the iconic Land's End to John O'Groats route. One such interaction is with a lovely lady called Janice, aged 67. I envy Janice for many reasons: her bike is lighter (she has been staying in B&B's the entire way) and she has been doing lower mileage every day, and as a result, Janice has been having a mostly delightful time. She tells me to check out the beach in Bettyhill, where she has just enjoyed a lovely picnic – however I know that I still have 15 very hilly miles to go after Bettyhill so won't be stopping, lest I find myself unable to move again. I also envy her because she is nearly finished and is therefore feeling triumphant – whereas my journey has barely begun. My finish line is still so very far away.

All in all, I calculate that I lose over an hour by being

social. Which seems fairly insignificant until I near the end of the day and, feeling ready to drop, all I can think is that would have been an hour sooner when I could be in the shade, hydrating, refuelling and resting.

My tank starts to feel empty with 20 miles to go. This is precisely when two guys roll up next to me in a car as I'm slowly struggling up another seemingly never-ending hill, desperately shoving trail mix into my mouth, sweat cascading from my face and splashing down on to the bike and tarmac. At first, I think they must be checking if I'm OK because I'm moving so slowly so I automatically offer a muffled reply, with a mouthful of nuts: 'Yep, I'm fine. Just flagging a bit now – it's been a long day.' I stop and we continue to chat. I'm half glad for the rest, but also mindful that I really just want to crack on and get this never-ending day done with. It turns out they are making a documentary about a guy I passed earlier, cycling Land's End to John O'Groats on a Brompton. Would I be interested in a road-side interview? As politely as I can manage, I tell them I really need to get to where I'm going and I can't spare an hour to provide them with a sound bite for their documen-tary – my water is running low and I must push on. The driver looks at me apologetically as his passenger continues to aggressively press me for the interview, while saying that he'd obviously have to leave out the fact that I'm cycling so much further because it would ruin the 'impact' of their main subject, but otherwise I seem 'pretty interesting' and it would be great to feature a girl, if I wouldn't mind down-playing the scale of my own challenge and also, ideally, say how inspired I was by the man on the Brompton.

My low blood sugar and mild dehydration is by now making me cranky and I channel every last bit of British politeness I can manage to resist just screaming expletives in response to his obnoxious refusal to get the hint and, frankly, rather patronising attitude. Eventually, the driver offers me one last apology and they speed off into the distance. Alone once more, I spend the next ten minutes angrily stewing and thinking of all the witty remarks I should have made and I then feel irrationally furious at myself for not being more assertive in getting them to leave sooner. More time wasted and still so far to go. Will this day never end?

The final ten miles are spent very deep in my pain cave. By the time I eventually crawl into Tongue, I am a broken woman, utterly exhausted from the long, sweaty slog. At least now I feel able to cry without holding back, knowing that I can at least rehydrate afterwards.

I get off my bike, eagerly anticipating the thoroughly indulgent pity party I'm about to throw for myself, when I hear another friendly hello from a couple of passing cyclists behind me. I turn around to say hello back, only to see two friends of mine, Kev and Vicky, who are also currently riding around the North Coast 500 route. I'd recommended it to them months before so I knew they were vaguely in the vicinity but the chances of us bumping into each other were so very slim, it hadn't really crossed my mind since. Had I stuck to my original timings for the day, we definitely would have missed each other.

The moment I realise who it is, I become overcome with joy which I unintentionally express by screaming like a banshee (causing a few locals to wonder what the commotion is) and nearly burst into tears. I immediately go from utterly wretched to feeling like the luckiest girl in Scotland – I couldn't have asked for a better day to see some friendly faces. I scream at least twice more, unable to hold in my excitement, and we hug (several times). Kev then buys each of us an ice cream which we eat whilst sitting on a bench as we have a little chat. Then we hug some more and part ways. Whilst my day was just finishing and I would now be scouting for a place to set up camp, their more relaxed schedule meant they were only just starting out – making sure to pick up a bottle of wine for later as a top priority before going anywhere. That night, I say a quiet thank you to the universe for the magical and surreal timing that allowed me to see and hug these friends of mine on a day I felt so low. It was the perfect gift.

The next morning, the sound of the wind angrily howling wakes me up in my tent in the small hours and provides an early warning that I'm in for another arduous day. The Scottish Highlands begin to feel like my very own Groundhog Day/torture chamber.

It is the next day that I throw what can only be described as a tantrum by the side of the road – unreasonably taking the fierce headwind situation very personally. I called Mum, looking for sympathy: 'I'm going the opposite way round to last time, the wind is rigged to make sure I always suffer!' I explain.

'The wind just does its thing, Laura,' she soothingly replies.

For the life of me I cannot understand why she doesn't see just how terribly unfair it all is.

'The OPPOSITE direction.' I emphasise. 'I SHOULD have a tail wind. It's literally NEVER a tail wind!' I continue, determined to prove that I am being personally persecuted by the weather.

Getting no support whatsoever for my wind conspiracy theory from Mum, I hang up feeling very frustrated. Then, instead of brooding on the unfairness of it all, I tried a new tactic that is much more effective. I cranked up the volume of my playlist and began serenading the local farm animals with some Taylor Swift: 'Cause the players gonna play, play, play, play, play / And the haters gonna hate, hate, hate, hate, hate . . .'

I then imagine Helga the Headwind once more feeling totally indignant that, despite her best efforts, she is unable to crush my spirits and this makes me sing louder in happy defiance: 'Baby, I'm just gonna shake, shake, shake, shake, shake I shake it off, I SHAKE IT OFF.'

When I'd had enough of that, I turned to the Beastie Boys and pretended that I was, in fact, starring in my very own music video. This is definitely what winning felt like. The ability to forcibly change my mood through singing (/very questionable rapping) becomes a vital coping strategy for the tough terrain. I force myself to find it funny when I am sent through a field when foolishly trusting Google maps for navigation. If there had been a recognisable bike path here once upon a time, it has now been undeniably reclaimed by nature. A couple of days ago this would have caused my mood to plummet, but instead I sing through this, too.

Bumping along through the wild and overgrown grass, panniers and various bits bouncing, I feel capable and Dory feels strong and reliable. Even though the last two hours of the day are a struggle, the rest of the day had felt doable and for that I feel grateful. With the sun still shining, I pitch my tent on a grass verge near to the sea in Banff. Home assembled, I run in to the North Sea for a bracing swim – nature's ice bath for fatigued legs.

MSR have contributed to my adventures once more and this time had provided me with a water filter, which meant I'd been able to pump plenty of safe drinking water from a nearby stream into my water bottles shortly before stopping.

I laugh at the memory of dribbling out saliva-heavy water through my mouth for cooking with on that first morning in Russia three years ago – some lessons are learnt the hard way! I successfully cook up some rice on my trusty stove and treat myself to a sachet of instant hot chocolate for dessert. Despite tiredness, I find it hard to sleep because I just want to soak up the perfect scenery. I've slept in some questionable places whilst adventuring but this spot is a gem. I love that only my bike and my legs have brought me to this idyllic moment. I eventually snuggle up in my sleeping bag and contentedly drift asleep to the sound of crashing waves nearby.

The next couple of days are what pain feels like – I get annihilated. Whatever good grace was once to be found, there is no sign of it on the final stretch along the Scottish coast. It hurts. A merciless headwind combines with fierce heat which makes for a bewildering combination that slowly but surely wears me down.

'Cheer up, it might never happen,' a man merrily suggests to me as he passes me struggling to load up the bike by the side of the road one morning.

Once again, I feel like crying when it's time to load up the bike with the panniers. Clearly, the feeling of this act is written all over my face. I regularly torture myself with thoughts about ceremoniously ditching the extra weight and zooming off, unburdened, into the sunset.

'Oh, that's just my concentration face!' I reply, trying to make a joke out of it. But it wasn't. I am filled with dread. Turning back to the bike, I softly whisper, 'I'm sorry, Dory. I'm not happy either,' pleading with her. She doesn't respond.

The limited energy in my tank is dwindling. I all but crawl up the final few hills. The heat, the wind, the seemingly ceaseless climbing uphill – it's breaking my spirit, chipping away at it piece by piece. It's hard to enjoy the views when everything hurts and you have to doggedly pedal forwards non-stop against the constant headwind to gain slow progress. For many of my days, I'm travelling at 6mph. It is soul destroying. Usually the day is written all over my face by the time I've finished – bloodshot eyes, pockets of sunburn dotted around the few places my Aethic suncream either missed or sweated off. I look battle worn and exhausted – which I am.

In Dundee, I am joined by Matt Gibson – who has found me via Instagram – and his bike, Lily. On the morning I'm due to cycle with Matt, I wake up feeling achy, tired and like a reluctant child that doesn't want to go to school. Morning yoga does little to appease my angry legs and I fear I'm in for a long battle with them today. I cringe at the thought of how slow I will be compared to Matt, who I know is a strong cyclist.

I meet him and discover he cycled 190 miles the day before and will in fact be cycling 200 miles back to Leeds the day after. It instantly makes me feel a bit pathetic for moaning about my tired legs, but Matt is unfailingly gracious, constantly sympathetic and encouraging. We laugh all day – *Anchorman* quotes and nutrition tips are swapped (we agree that Orange Fanta and pizza is the pro fuel of choice) and when, six miles out from Edinburgh, I get a puncture, Matt valiantly fixes it in about two minutes – using his own spare inner tube as a donation to the cause. Matt will later also donate some replacement bike parts for Dory before I head over to Europe and regularly send over encouragement during the rest of the weeks on the road. Friendships forged in sweat are a special kind.

Throughout the day, we see dozens of other cyclists out

enjoying the sunshine – I envy all of them for having such light bikes. In my head, I imagine Dory bitterly grumbling away about the situation, too: 'None of those other road bikes are weighed down, Laura . . . Look how much quicker they're going.'

I imagine the other bikes calling out to her in sympathy, much as their riders sometimes do as they pass me going up a hill: 'I can barely get myself up this hill, I don't know how you manage with all that weight on it!' says one particularly cheerful gent as he slowly but inevitably passes me.

As the heatwave continues to blast across the UK, I produce mini waterfalls of sweat throughout the day. I feel disgusting. I am also very aware that after a few days of sweating in the fierce Scottish hills, my clothes are really beginning to smell. If even I'm aware of my stench, I dread to think how bad it is for other people – in this case, Matt. He says he cannot smell it but I'm sure he is just being polite.

Nearing Edinburgh, I get desperate for the pizza we were talking about earlier in the day. 'What we need is a pizza,' I say. And at that very moment, we spot an Italian restaurant – naturally, we take it as a hallowed sign from the universe. We laugh some more. Ordering a starter and a main each, we both devour the food and all but lick our plates clean. Matt's generosity shines through once more as he insists on paying the bill. By the time we hug each other goodbye, Matt feels more like an old friend than a stranger I met for the first time a few hours ago.

I realise I am smiling when I get back to my cheap hotel. Connections like these, no matter how small, are ones I treasure on the road. With long days spent craving comfort and missing friends and family back home, it's hugely reassuring to connect with someone else who understands all the complicated emotions that an endurance challenge can bring to the surface; the call of adventure and longing for freedom that perpetually wrestle with the pangs of home-sickness. I often wondered if I'd ever find the right balance.

Normally, by the time I make it to my rest day accommodation, I slump straight onto the bed in an exhausted heap but today has been FUN. The simple act of human company goes a long way and I feel both ready to drop and reinvigorated all at once. The day has injected me with a new lease of enthusiasm.

All the same, my legs immediately start to seize up as I bask on the bed and finish off some more chocolate before crashing out. Tomorrow's rest day mission will be to find a laundrette, but for today, I am done. The next time I hit the road, it will be to head back to England. A thought that cheers me up immediately. I will be sad to leave Scotland but it's nice to feel like I'm heading back home and also leaving the infamous hills of Scotland behind. Progress!

Utterly exhausted, I sleep like the dead but wake up the next morning feeling the puzzling combination of extreme fatigue and restlessness. Spending the day with Matt yesterday has made me realise just how isolated I've been. After two weeks on the road, I have somewhat underestimated the effects of loneliness but it starts to creep in around me like a thick fog in that hotel room in Edinburgh. I can't put a finger on why I feel so low and why eating all the calories I can manage isn't cheering me up as much as it normally does, but I have a foolproof plan that I know will cheer me up – I will call Dad, who will undoubtedly be armed with any number of completely awful jokes to snap me out of my grump.

I video call him and am greeted by the image of him lying in a hospital bed. My stomach churns and the colour immediately drains from my face. Typical Dad, he acts like nothing has happened, or is even slightly out of the ordinary.

'Hello, sweetheart. You all right?' he says.

'What's happened?!' comes my quick reply.

'You having a rest day today? How are you feeling?' he softly asks.

'Yeah, Dad, I'm OK. What's happened?' I repeat.

'Kidney stones,' he replies. I breathe a sigh of relief that it's not more serious, but I still feel a pang of guilt for feeling even slightly sorry for myself.

He continues to ask me about the trip and I continue to try and press him for more information. He reveals he will hopefully only be in there for a couple of days – if he doesn't pass the stones naturally by then, he'll need surgery. But, ever the optimist, he expects confidently to pass them. I ask him how he is and he admits, reluctantly, that it's painful. He shows me his arm linked up to an intravenous drip in response to my question of 'Can they do anything for the pain?' The conversation is brief as I'm aware of him being in discomfort and I'm also stunned. He reassures me that I needn't worry and tells me he's following my tracker map all the way. He says we'll speak in a couple of days, although I know I will of course be checking in on him the next day. As soon as the call ends, I burst into tears. Loud, sobbing, uncontrollable tears.

The sight of my cheerful, cheeky dad lying vulnerable in hospital has tipped me over the edge and the fleeting loneliness and isolation of the past couple of weeks is now all at once acute. I am desperately homesick. Dad lives in Istanbul anyway, so in reality I'm no further from him than usual, but it feels so much worse. All at once I feel selfish and I miss my family. My wonderful, ever-supportive family. Who apparently, even when in severe pain, make sure to cheer me on and tell me to 'rest up', and to congratulate me on doing so brilliantly so far.

When I first started adventures, it was a way of escaping a life I wasn't proud of and didn't enjoy much. These days, life is on a much better track and I sometimes feel that makes it harder to leave. But equally, I'm not quite content enough to stay put for too long either. I wonder if I'd ever find a happy middle ground. That night is the first I struggle to sleep since the challenge began – my physical exhaustion outmatched by my vigorous mental gymnastics. Over and over I picture Dad in his hospital room in Istanbul and wish I could somehow teleport myself there just to give him a hug.

After barely sleeping, I don't want to begin the next day and I audibly moan when my alarm inevitably signals that it's time to be on the move once more. I wearily make my way out of Edinburgh feeling totally frazzled. I struggle to rally and the gloomy morning fog as I pedal out of Edinburgh matches my mood perfectly. The sun soon glares down and burns through the fog, leaving me reminiscing nostalgically about the novel sensation of being too cold earlier that morning.

Rivers of sweat once again pour down me as I steadily climb hill after hill, after hill. My tank feels empty and I keep needing to pee, my body now feeling like it's fighting some kind of virus. Hotter and hotter, up and up we climb.

There is no singing on the bike today – I fear that if I make any noise, the floodgates will open and the tears I'm desperately holding back will all come tumbling out. I quietly pedal onwards, resigned to my fate. The downhills that usually offer such childlike fun instead make me freezing cold. The heavy climbs uphill keep me warm but exhaust me. I cannot win today. Please, let it be over.

I listen to *Home* by Phillip Phillip on repeat, all day.

'Just know you're not alone
"Cause I'm going to make this place your home'

Over and over I listen to it, desperately trying to comfort myself with the reassuring lyrics. Today is, after all, also the day I will pass over the border to England. Home.

By late afternoon, however, I can't fight my emotions any longer and I find myself on the side of the road, sobbing. It's just too hard, the bike is too heavy and I'm ready to break. After two weeks on the road, I'm infuriated that my body is struggling this much and hasn't yet adapted. I feel empty – my legs are wrecked, my mind is a mess. When I at last pass over the border, it is a relief to see England but I barely pause long enough to take a photo of the sign that marks the landmark before carrying onwards to Berwick, desperate to finish for the day and rest. I fall asleep at 8pm and remain feverish throughout the night. I reluctantly wake at 7am the next morning, drenched in sweat in my sleeping bag, to try it all again.

Welcome back to England! A thick fog lurks all day and the visibility is, at best, horrendous. Once again getting caught out by the fickle nature of British 'cycle' paths, the first hour of the day is spent slipping and sliding over mud and gravel – not all bike paths are created equal. I worry that Dory's tires are getting shredded but, more than that, barely able to see anything in the soupy atmosphere, I cynically mull over the chances of us both accidentally sliding off the nearby cliff. After eventually getting through to a road I perk up, but when Google maps tries to send me through another field a few minutes later I snap and decide to take matters into my own hands. I decide I've had enough of this particular section of the official bike route and I turn the bike around, instead opting for the horrendously busy A1 road instead. Yes, it'll be noisy and busy but I reason that it'll be quicker in the long run because it'll be on tarmac.

Lorries rattle past, cars and caravans speed by – the majority of caravans as per usual passing too closely. I focus on just keeping my head down to crank the miles out. I console myself by thinking that, what with all the fog, the visibility on the 'scenic' route would have been awful anyway. Every now and then a lorry passes so close to me that I feel uncomfortably aware of my own mortality. It's mostly terrifying and I never relax, but I do make progress. That is all I care about today – progress. Getting to Newcastle as soon as physically possible so I can crawl back to sleep.

With the hard shoulder of the busy dual carriageway being littered with various bits of glass and debris, I unsurprisingly get my second puncture – a situation that unexpectedly makes me utterly hysterical. Swearing and sobbing, ranting and wailing as the traffic thunders past. I become convinced I can't change the tyre, despite having done it countless times before, and, having had enough, I call a cab. By the time he arrives I have been on the side of the road for over an hour and I'm shivering. I also have successfully changed the tyre. I don't know why I became so convinced I'd messed it up, but it was the final straw. I feel hugely guilty at missing 25 miles, promising myself I will make them up somehow. But I also feel relieved. I am beyond exhausted and my legs are like lead. This A road is no place to be for a cyclist – the many close calls throughout the day have no doubt contributed to the hysterics.

The taxi driver, Brian, is both amazed and appalled I'm

on the road to begin with. Warm hearted and friendly, Brian insists that we stop for a hot chocolate and a toasted sandwich in a petrol station, as I clearly look every bit as cold as I feel. Back in the car, he tells me a story about his own cycling struggles – he recently cycled 40 minutes to the pub with his son, which turned into three hours on the way back because of the huge hill. 'It seemed like such a nice idea until that bloody hill,' he jokes. It's a sentiment I empathise with fully. He then goes on to recommend some places for dinner by the river in Newcastle. I don't have the heart to tell him that I will be getting a cheap dinner from the supermarket and eating it as quickly as possible before passing out. I've stopped caring about the sights to see. I'm just trying to get through it.

I get to sleep at 8:30. Feeling jaded, tired and grumpy, I no longer even recognise myself. I have become a perpetually miserable and tired creature – living only to sleep, dreading time on the bike. I feel guilty for not enjoying it more, but more than anything, I desperately just want a rest period longer than 24 hours. How tremendous it would be to have two whole days! I wish I'd given myself a bit more leeway with the schedule and my timings.

The next day once again begins with low motivation and this sets the tone for another miserable, strife-filled day. The 'bike route' is more of an obstacle course. First I have to haul Dory up some stairs to cross a bridge and then I have to somehow haul her over a fence. I lose it, again. Sobbing, tired, miserable – completely irrational. To get us through the fence I have to take everything off Dory, launch the bags over the top and then lift the unencumbered bike high above my head and shimmy through. It's too much. I rant and rave into the air with only horses nearby to hear, who show little sympathy with my situation. It crosses my mind that if the farmer is near enough to hear my angry mono-logue, he will most likely think that I'm mentally deranged, but I no longer care.

Bike reloaded, I wheel us through and then I'm hit by another fence that requires me to repeat the farce all over again. More frustrated and furious crying ensues. I feel ready to break. Cursing the 'bike route' yet again I lose patience and opt for another busy A road.

With 40 miles left to go, and just four and a half hours into the day, I have nothing left. Whether through sheer exhaustion or some sort of food poisoning, I have been unable to keep food down since hitting the main road and after three hours of repeatedly vomiting, I'm completely broken. Mum calls me for a catch up whilst I'm on the busy A road and upon hearing the state I'm in, suggests I get the train to Whitby. Reluctantly, I agree.

I'm a couple of miles out from Hartlepool train station when she calls back to tell me that she's helpfully checked the timetable and the next train isn't actually until 5pm, which will get me to my destination for 7:30pm. For the second time in as many days, I erupt into angry, frustrated and exhausted tears. Totally overwrought and unable to think clearly, I decide that if I had just somehow stayed on the road, somehow just limped on instead of diverting to the train station – I would have theoretically been there for 4pm.

It's all too much. Still unable to digest food and totally frazzled, the thought of getting to Whitby at 7:30pm – 12 hours after setting off – is more than I can handle. In desperation, I once again call a taxi. I pass out instantly in the back seat and don't wake up until we get to Whitby, where I've booked last minute into a B&B. I am a level of worn out I've never known. Getting to the top of the stairs in the B&B feels like an achievement in its own right. I venture out only once to get a large pizza and a large cheesy garlic bread, which I eat in my room, and then fall asleep immediately after, thankfully managing at last to keep food down.

Thirteen hours of sleep later, I still don't feel 100 per cent, but I do feel just about well enough to continue, so that's what I do. The first couple of hours on the road are once again bleak and foggy, and feature the by now standard Google map jokes of sending me through a load of mud (classic), a SAND PIT (ridiculous), up two separate 16 per cent inclines (so much ouch) and, of course, along a couple of busy A roads when I get fed up of faffing around. (Soon after this, I would discover a route planning app called *Komoot*, which was deigned specifically for cycling and hiking - and therefore much better suited to the task in hand!) I think I might have made a mistake getting back on the bike but thankfully my body remembers how to digest food so I just keep refuelling and keep on going.

At 2pm, I stop at a service station to eat as much as I can before pushing on for the second half of the day. Milkshake, vegetable pasty, ice cream – it all goes in. But I am in for a pleasant surprise! Fuelled by ice cream, I find myself on some blissfully quiet B roads and the sun even makes a couple of appearances! More than ever, I'm convinced that ice cream is medicinal, so I have another two scoops (banoffee and mint chocolate chip) that night just to be on the safe side. I finish feeling weary, but infinitely better than the past couple of days. At long last, it's happening – I feel my body adapting.

The next day, I remember to smile and I also remember that I know how to do this. It feels like I'm finally emerging from under a dark cloud that I feared would never leave.

Riding over the Humber Bridge, I am grinning from ear to ear. I've always loved bridges and there's just something about cycling over them in particular that always fills me with joy. My dad later tells me that my Grandad Norman had actually helped to build the Humber Bridge. I bet at the time he had no idea his granddaughter would years later be riding across it. Especially not the same hysterical granddaughter he had to frequently rescue from spiders! Admittedly, I still wasn't great with spiders, but Dad says he would have been proud of the brave woman I'd grown up to be all the same.

The next day, I am once again joined by a new friend made via social media. Ian Preedy accompanies me on the blissfully flat ride from Lincolnshire to Kings Lynn. I'm reminded how much faster the miles go when you have someone to chat away to. Ian kindly brings some chocolate and doesn't seem to mind when I stop for lunch at 10:30am. I am, however, devastated when the local petrol station doesn't have a milkshake. The guy behind the counter sympathises: 'I know, right? I eat these flapjacks for breakfast every morning – they'd go lovely with a milkshake.' I get a Solero ice cream instead, much to Ian's amusement as it's before noon and not exactly what you'd consider to be typical ice cream weather: it's grey and misty outside, and our waterproof layers have been close to hand all morning.

Arriving into Kings Lynn, I pop into Richardsons Cycles, the local bike shop, to replace my bike lock – in a state of delirium a few days ago at Hartlepool station, I'd left mine behind. I am greeted by Stefan, the friendliest bike mechanic I've ever met.

I usually pass out as soon as I get into bed, but that night I have trouble falling asleep. It suddenly dawns on me that, for once, I'm not completely exhausted! My legs are tight but they are adapting, and I'm smiling. Finally, I'm finding my rhythm and I feel like I'm where I need to be. I get even more excited when I get up to check the route ahead and realise that I've only got two days left before I'll be at my mum's house.

As a coping strategy, I've been focusing on one day at a time and deliberately not considering the bigger picture of the challenge – any time I did think about how far I still had left to go, it became overwhelming. Therefore, it is only just starting to sink in, as I sit in the launderette in Kings Lynn the next day, that I've all but finished the UK section of the ride. Day by day, mile by mile, it has all added up and slowly, but surely, I've made progress. Just a few days ago I was at my absolute limit and desperate for a rest, but miraculously I now feet energised and ready. I hope this is the start of a new chapter.

On the final approach to Mum's home in Essex, I start to recognise the roads and begin uncontrollably yelling into the air, much to the bemusement of the local drivers. It feels utterly surreal that after setting off from the most northerly part of the UK just under a month ago, I am now once again on these roads I know so well from days of training; the roads that have provided hours of headspace. It's a huge comfort not to worry about navigation and to be tantalisingly close to home. I'm dreaming of my bed and several cups of MumTea (everyone knows that mums make the best cups of tea). I still have a way to go yet but I'm definitely ready for a couple of days to recharge and relax.

As it turns out, there isn't actually huge amount of time to either relax or recharge because there is a flurry of admin to catch up on, including getting the bike serviced and myself booked in for a sports massage, and repacking! I've been chatting with various friends adept at lightweight bikepacking, and I'm now determined to go much lighter for the European section.

Being rather ignorant about bike mechanics, I'd had no idea that you could get different gearing ratios that would help with hills – Matt had pointed this out within the first hour of our ride to Edinburgh and we both laughed at how much harder I'd unintentionally made things for myself. With this new knowledge, I was also determined to change my gearing during the layover, too. I come home to find that Matt had actually also posted over some bike upgrades to help me on my way, including a new bike pump and cassette. As with many other challenges, though this was a solo journey, I am by no means by myself – this small act of kindness buoys me up and adds to the motivation to continue.

There is also the very important matter of meeting my nephew Freddy, who was born the day I left to go to Aberdeen. I get home from a sports massage and, despite there being tons to do before I leave again in 24 hours' time, I decide that all of it will just have to wait whilst I cuddle my nephew. I'd congratulated my brother through intermittent phone signal as the train sped towards Aberdeen and I had felt sad to not be around for Freddy's birth. Thankfully, the latest addition to the Kennington family seems to have forgiven me and promptly falls asleep on me, dribbling just a little bit.

Also forming the welcome party at my mum's house are my two older brothers, my other nephew and my five nieces. Having so desperately missed my family, I'm soaking up the brilliantly chaotic family time and mentally trying to bank the love and cuddles from my nieces and nephews – who frequently pile on me all at once – for later on.

I'm acutely aware of how much mentally tougher the

next section is likely to be, with the various language barriers and the added complications they inevitably bring. This European section brings so many more unknowns and, packing up to leave again, my stomach is once more in knots.

A DAY LATER, as I cycle from Mum's to Tilbury Docks to get the ferry to Gravesend, the bike is lighter but my heart feels heavy. All over again, it all feels impossible – the challenge ahead is so much bigger than the challenges behind me. To even get this far took everything I had. How much more do I have left to give? Do I have enough? It doesn't feel like it. I feel small and nervous.

Thankfully, I am joined by Sian and Adam at Tilbury – more new friends courtesy of social media – who are accompanying me for part of the final UK section to Dover. Both keep me laughing all day and I'm relieved to have had the distraction from the butterflies that have been causing an internal cyclone in my stomach. By the time they leave, the butterflies have calmed down and I remind myself to simply take this section – like all the sections before it – one day, one mile and one pedal stroke at a time. I have friends in the Netherlands so I focus on getting to them and tell myself to worry about the irrational sense of impending doom and loneliness later.

The next day sees an early morning ferry ride over to Dunkirk. Once again, the adventure fairies seem to have a little trick up their sleeve. As I untie Dory from the rails of the ferry and get her ready to disembark, I find myself next to two other cyclists – the cheerful Adele and Cam, both originally from Australia but currently residing in the UK.

It turns out that they're heading to Bruges on a weekend holiday and, whilst I'm headed further that day, to just past the border of the Netherlands, we're all headed in the same direction so we instantly agree to ride together. I inwardly smile at the irony; my deep concern about being lonely in Europe seems to have been dismantled within minutes of arriving in France.

Greeted immediately by Helga the headwind, we ride as a group and take it in turns to be up at the front, shielding the others from the wind. Adele and Cam generously insist on doing the bulk of this but even still, with their lighter bikes – they have one rucksack each in stark contrast to my somewhat lighter but still fully loaded bike – it's a big effort to keep up with their pace. Regardless, it's nice to be part of a team, and I'm thankful for the company – a welcome distraction from the nerves still bubbling just under the surface.

When they stop in a quaint little town in Belgium for lunch, I opt to carry on – somewhat envious of their relaxed schedule and lower mileage, once again pondering if I'm doing this cycle touring malarkey all wrong when nearly everyone else I meet seems to be on a much more pleasant time frame. For the rest of the day on the road, I daydream about how lovely it would be to wake up later, have a long lunch and cycle leisurely through Europe. The lines of one my favourite poems by Robert Frost would always resound in my head in retaliation to this fantasy:

'The woods are lovely, dark and deep,

But I have promises to keep,

And miles to go before I sleep'

I do have miles to go and promises to keep. I remind myself that this isn't a holiday, it is a challenge. The standards I'd set out to uphold and the promises I'd made were to myself, but they still mattered. If you don't hold yourself accountable, who will?

On I pedal into the ceaseless headwind, eventually reaching my target at 8:30pm after some surprise road closures added an extra 17 kilometres to the end of the day, when I should have had just five kilometres left. Ouch.

The next day, I am headed to KEEN Europe HQ in Rotterdam, the first of two friendly stops in the Netherlands. Over the years of working with KEEN, they've become more like good friends than brand partners and it feels great to be cycling towards familiar faces. After the many hills of Scotland and England, I'd been daydreaming about these flat roads for weeks – picturing blissful, easy miles. Naively, not once did I consider that I'd have a 19mph headwind to contend with – nicknamed the 'Dutch mountains' by the locals – that would make the flat roads an absolute misery. There is no escape from Helga's merciless onslaught.

It is especially painful on the sections that run directly alongside the coast – the wind whips the nearby sand into a frenzy and it regularly feels like I'm being aggressively slapped in the face by millions of tiny, angry grains of wrath personified. I do my best to cheerfully consider it as some sort of weird beauty treatment when it's time to rub more sun cream on to my sand covered and sweaty face – au naturel exfoliation, anyone? No expense spared – ears included for free!

After also experiencing the grit of sand repeatedly crunching between my teeth, caused by unintentionally inviting in yet more sand as I smile back at the cheerful locals as I pass them, I decide that it's best to cover up completely. I put my sunglasses on and pull up my buff over my nose, the latter feeling (and no doubt looking) ridiculous in such hot weather.

My ETA to meet Maren from KEEN becomes later and later and when I do finally arrive, I am totally spent. KEEN have kindly put me up in a hotel near the office for the next couple of nights and I quickly check in, planning to have a brief shower before heading out with Maren for dinner. The hotel itself is incredibly trendy and glamorous – a far cry from the budget options I'd been staying in for my rest days and I feel somewhat out of place with my slightly smelly lycra and my cleated bike shoes click-clicking all over the stone floor. I needn't have worried though, this is the Netherlands after all – a cycling haven (when the wind behaves!) and all cyclists are welcome here.

I get up to my room to discover it is in fact less of a room and more of a small apartment. It takes up two floors: there's a small kitchen area and a gigantic bath tub on the ground floor, with a king-size bed and a small sofa on the second floor. I spend a couple of minutes just marvelling at the sheer size of it. I can't help but laugh in astonishment at the audacious luxury of it all. I feel like a princess – a dishevelled, weary and stinky princess, but a princess all the same.

A very quick shower later, and Maren and I head out for dinner. Having arrived much later than planned, I'm ravenous and desperate for anything even remotely edible. After a 40-minute walk into the centre of Rotterdam, I'm practically ready to eat the furniture. We opt for a local pizza restaurant that Maren knows and it doesn't disappoint – both pizzas are huge, delicious and packed full of fresh ingredients. I polish mine off within minutes – and then eat the rest of Maren's when she is unable to finish it. A waiter looks on slightly amazed (and I'd like to think also quite impressed) that someone so small is able to eat so much.

After catching up on all the various bits of life gossip, Maren kindly escorts me back to the hotel and we arrange to catch up again tomorrow. I dive into my huge, comfy bed and fall asleep with a smile on my face. Moments like this are to be treasured.

The next day, the comfy king size bed holds me hostage; I'm trapped in a fluffy prison of wonderment, helpless to resist the duvet's demands to snuggle down just a little longer. It is only my hunger that eventually drives me to get moving. I stock up on a huge breakfast in the hotel before getting on with the few bits of admin I need to do that day, which includes restocking my food and doing some laundry, the latter of which is accomplished once again thanks to KEEN, who have an apartment just above their offices with a washing machine they let me use. As I wait for the wash cycle to complete, I have a nap on the sofa. The rest of the day follows a similarly lazy tone – I eat, I sleep, I have a bath and then I eat some more before it's time to crawl back into bed for the night. A feeling of contentedness settles in as I drift off. Europe: so far, so good.

My legs are groggy to start the next day but soon find a rhythm. In the slightly modified words of famous rapper Jay Z, I had 99 problems, but inconsiderate motorists weren't one – the incredible Dutch cycle infrastructure is a thing of beauty. Young, old, little or large – everyone is on their bikes. I have totally fallen in love with the cycle culture and wish the UK would take note.

It's an easy spin out to the coast and I arrive earlier than planned, so rather than wait for it to get dark and scout for a place to wild camp, I treat myself to a cheap cabin in an official campsite nearby, which, much to my delight, comes with its very own outside hammock. The campsite is huge and even has its own restaurant, though mindful of saving money, I instead opt to raid the local supermarket where I reason I can consume an outrageous amount of calories without spending too much. It's very much about quantity and not so much about quality. As a starter, I cover four ready made pancakes with chocolate spread, and then heat up some instant noodles. Before they're cooked I've also eaten a ball of fresh mozzarella and a pack of smoked salmon.

This becomes my standard dinner most nights if I manage to find a supermarket – prioritising fat and maximising calories whenever possible. Although I obviously can't keep fresh vegetables cool on the bike I always try to buy a cucumber (high water content and high in fibre!) to snack on during the day and then add in fresh vegetables as regularly as possible amidst the rest of the calorie dense food. Though I still stick to a largely vegan diet when home, I worry about restricting my food options during challenges. Although eating tonnes of food sound, I usually needed way more calories than I'm physically able to consume anyway. Eating that much food sometimes feels like a chore, and I am also once more mindful of local hospitality that might include meat/fish.

The next day, I am greeted by a phenomenon as rare as it is wonderful – Helga the Headwind's younger, sexier and altogether more charming sister, Tina the Tailwind! A couple of navigational mishaps (Google maps strikes again!) mean that it's a wiggly start to the morning (with some minor accidental trespassing also featuring) but at a whopping 27mph, the wind is mostly blowing in my favour and I feel invincible as Dory and I zoom along. We pass through a peaceful nature reserve, where water buffalo occasionally block our path, and from there continue along the coast. I feel rather smug when I pass the many cyclists battling away in the other direction, the struggle I know all too well written all over their faces. It's a glorious day for me but undoubtedly torturous for them. I savour being on this side of the equation for once.

That night I'm staying with my friend Ned Aufenfast on the island of Texel. The first and only time I'd met Ned was years beforehand; we were both headed to the Adventure Travel Film Festival to help Dave Cornthwaite run a stand. The plan had been for Ned to pick me up and then we'd pick up Dave en route a couple of hours later. Unfortunately, Ned and I got stuck in severe traffic on a motorway for several hours, meaning Dave sadly never joined the road trip and instead had to haul his books and gear across a couple of trains and in a taxi – he couldn't afford to be late because he was in fact speaking that opening night at the event. After spending most of the day in a car together, my friendship with Ned had been accelerated – much to Dave's amusement, we were both mildly hysterical and giggling uncontrollably by the time we eventually turned up to the festival. I don't think either of us could have told you what was so funny but as first meetings go, it was memorable.

Car journeys with Ned prove to be a reliable formula for hysteria: he shows me around the island of Texel, narrating various points of interests as a newly invented alter ego, the smooth radio presenter of Ned FM. We once again find ourselves violently laughing at not much at all. Discovering that Texel is a mecca for kitesurfing and outrageous chocolate brownies, I'm sad to be only here for an evening and add the island to the ever-growing list of places to return to. Ned drives me out to the top of the island to catch a phenomenal sunset – we are both silent for once and in awe as the uninterrupted horizon dazzles in varying degrees of orange and pink. It's 1am by the time we eventually go to sleep that night – hours past my usual bedtime and I know I'll be feeling tired the next day, but I'm also grateful to be soaking up the company whilst I can.

With its incredible cycle infrastructure and the fact that everyone speak English, I suspect the Netherlands has rather spoiled me for the weeks ahead, but I'm thankful for the easy re-introduction to life on the road. If there is one complaint, it is about the endlessly flat roads. Although I'd initially been so excited for them, my view on them has now started to range from 'a bit tedious' to 'absolute hell', depending on the wind's speed and direction. I develop a worryingly angry niggle in my right leg and do my best not to consider that I still have four more countries to ride through.

I further exacerbate things when, four miles before the end of my final day in the Netherlands, I ride over some temporary metal plates, which somehow slip and send both me and the bike skidding sideways into some nearby gravel at 18mph. The actual physical damage to me and the bike is fairly minimal – I seem to have a bruised leg and pelvis, plus a few scrapes that I clean out, whilst Dory's right shifter has bent inward. The emotional reaction is stronger – I burst into tears, feeling about five years old, before then turning my frustration towards the metal plates, giving them a thorough telling off. I then break into my emergency chocolate and slowly complete the final four miles of the day.

I miss the official border marking the next day, but when I find myself surrounded by German flags I realise I've reached a new country. Five minutes after spotting the flags, I see a man doing various elaborate arm exercises whilst walking vigorously. Less than an hour later, I see a very stern man in a bright neon outfit rollerblading – very seriously. Both resemble something out of a Monty Python sketch and make me giggle.

The road surface seems to have suddenly become incredibly bumpy and, as I rattle towards the small town of Dornum, I instantly feel nostalgic for the blissful cycle paths of the Netherlands a few miles away. Promising myself to not judge so soon, I hold out hope that Germany might have some pleasant tricks up its sleeves yet. Everything is closed in Dornum when I arrive, Sundays being an eerily quiet affair in this part of Germany, but Google maps finally redeems itself and I find a nearby pizzeria that is open. I order a gigantic pizza that costs me all of five euros and consider it a fitting celebration for reaching country number five.

It's fair to say that Germany and I don't get off to a good start. Unlike the bout of loneliness that slowly crept in around me whilst I was in Scotland, loneliness hits all at once and like a ton of bricks on my first morning in Germany. Instantly, the challenge feels unachievable and like a rollercoaster ride I can't get off. I miss my family, I miss my friends and I curse my lack of (read: non-existent) German language skills.

The next day, it's grey and drizzly and Dory and I are once again rattling along the lumpy German paths. On the ferry to Bremerhaven, a guy with several teeth missing insists on repeatedly winking and blowing kisses at me from his car and completely disregards my lack of interest. Thankfully, the ferry journey is only 20 minutes long – although it feels much, much longer. I arrive already a little on edge to hear sirens and, getting off the ferry, I spot what I suspect are various drug deals taking place. Having lived in London for many years, urban scenes aren't especially new to me but I feel distinctly uneasy very quickly.

I have booked into a cheap Airbnb in Bremerhaven for the night – days of cycling in the rain have left me wanting to thaw out both me and my kit. Finding the building, worn down and covered in graffiti, with yet more seemingly dodgy characters lurking nearby, I wonder if I have accidentally booked myself into a brothel or drug den – the price did seem a little too good. Thankfully, two more cyclists soon arrive, even though they are extremely grumpy, and we are also soon greeted by cheerful property owner Paolo. As jolly as he is, Paolo still sternly refuses to let me take my bike up to the room and - regardless of my protestations about security (or lack thereof) - he adamantly insists that we store our bikes in the building next door instead and that they will certainly be safe. I silently tell myself off for having an overactive imagination as we climb the stairs up to the rooms – the building is infinitely nicer on the inside than the exterior would have suggested, with a communal kitchen area on each floor, and my room is spacious, clean and bright.

I wake up the next morning determined to greet the day with positivity, but within the first couple of hours of being on the road, I'm already frustrated and feeling like Germany and I need a time out from one another. More incredibly bumpy cycle paths, more drizzle. I switch to the road in an attempt to find a smoother ride but it's only five (blissful) minutes before cars start beeping angrily at me for not being on the cycle path, despite there being plenty of room for us both.

Four minutes later, I get stopped by two very stern policemen for the heinous crime of being on the pavement – I'd apparently missed the subtle section of cycle path on the actual road. Just ahead of me, the cycle path goes back onto the very pavement I am currently on. As margins of error go, this one was very precise. The police officers also take the opportunity to tell me off for having both of my earphones in, regardless of my assurances that the volume was definitely low enough for me to hear any traffic. 'It is not allowed,' they repeat several times, in response to whatever I say. I consider telling them that not only do I think there are any number of more important things they could be addressing at this moment, but also that I've successfully cycled thousands of miles with my earphones in without causing injury to myself or others. I instead decide to politely smile and nod, agreeing to only put one earbud in and to pay very close attention to the cycle paths. Five minutes later, both earphones go back in – not least to distract me from the rattling of the bike over the many lumps, cracks and dips. I hate German cycle paths. Bump bump bump – it's going to be a long day.

Ten minutes after my chat with the local police, I go to overtake a woman walking her two Labradors on the cycle path. I ding my bell a few times as I approach but there's no reaction. I get closer and as I slow down and cheerfully say, 'Hello, sorry!' she responds by angrily shouting something at me in German. I have no idea what's she saying of course, but she's still shouting at me as I pedal on. Whatever cheery intentions I set out with in the morning are long gone now; I just want today to be over with.

I am still mildly stewing in my frustration and self-pity when I get to Cuxhaven, where suddenly everything gets better. The long-distance cycle path along the coast boasts beautiful views and I'm delighted to find the people walking along the path actually smile back at me! Never underestimate the gift of a smile. These simple friendly expressions lift me up more than the people offering them will ever know – the sense of loneliness I'm now feeling is palpable and I cherish every kind human interaction, no matter how small.

Sheep occasionally form an obstacle when they veer from the nearby grass onto the path, but at least this path is smooth. Although there is an illogical number of gates to get through and there is sheep poo scattered everywhere, compared to the morning, it's delightful. If there is one minor complaint it's that despite this being a well-advertised cycle path, I have to stop at least every 10–15 minutes to wiggle the bike through the gates. In my cynical state of mind, I muse over an elaborate conspiracy theory: I contemplate that whoever is in charge of the cycle infrastructure in Germany must really hate cyclists, perhaps having had his/her heart broken by one in the past, and now lives for subtle, petty revenge against all cyclist kind. I imagine them manically laughing to themselves as they implement yet more awkwardly placed gates or sabotage the cycle path surfaces with some sort of jackhammer. I ponder that, if they haven't done so already, they should make friends with the people responsible for the rather woeful British cycle infrastructure, too.

Much to my relief, I find myself on beautiful country lanes for the rest of the day. On the actual road! For days it's been frustrating to see smooth tarmac yet be forced to use the rickety bike paths, so I appreciate every minute on tarmac. Arriving into the beautifully quaint little town of Stade, I am greeted by sunshine and cobbles, and people dining outside, laughing and relaxing.

Doing my usual supermarket sweep for cheese and instant noodles, I go to get a basket and a security guard stops me to check my bag. Clearly, I've been marked as a criminal today! I amuse myself by thinking of the policemen from the morning issuing out a national alert: 'WARNING:

Have you seen this girl? She cycles with BOTH EARPHONES in and has been known to occasionally cycle IN THE ROAD! Considered extremely dangerous and untrustworthy.'

In the end, the supermarket – the size of a giant warehouse – proves too much for my frazzled brain. I find the nearest restaurant and order a giant plate of pasta instead.

The next night, after a little help from a friendly local man when I accidentally get on the wrong ferry (it had to happen sooner or later), I arrive into Hamburg, where my weekly rest day awaits. I'd been to Hamburg for speaking events and loved it, so I was looking forward to being somewhere familiar. Alas, my usual hunt for a cheap rest day hotel had, this time, totally backfired. The hostility of the staff upon check in set the tone; I assume they were very good friends with the embittered person in charge of Germany's cycle infrastructure and therefore shared a similar disdain for all cyclists.

I'm kept awake all night by the loud dance music blasting out from the bar opposite the hotel and the various street brawls that seem to be kicking off every few minutes. Every time I cautiously peek out of my window, I also see various prostitutes and drug dealers strutting up and down the street – this time, there is no chance my overactive imagination is to blame. I'm not religious but I pray that my beloved Dory is still here in the morning. Having been repeatedly told once more at check in a line I was coming to know well in Germany – that it was 'not allowed' to store her inside the hotel, I'd reluctantly left Dory in the underground car park beside the hotel. With nothing to lock her to, I'd had to leave her leaning against the wall near the office. The vague assurances of the car park warden are doing nothing to comfort me now and I don't sleep at all that night. I have become extremely protective over her, and after six weeks of sleeping with her next to me, I experience separation anxiety that she is so far away, particularly in such a rough neighbourhood.

The next morning, I make a decision to double the scheduled distance to get out of Germany a day quicker. I'm tired, grumpy and so perhaps unfairly focusing all of my grievances on Germany, but over the past few days, I've experienced so much hostility and repeatedly clashed with the abrupt and direct communication style of many Germans and I've had enough. I'm not blameless in this dynamic – I've undoubtedly misinterpreted harmless cultural differences due to overtiredness – but either way, I decide I need to leave. My mood has been spiralling since crossing into Germany and the smallest bump – literal or emotional – has usually triggered tears. It's completely irrational but I feel every accumulated mile now; my body and mind both feel jaded – not only from the physical distance but also the sense of isolation from having no one but myself to rely on all day, every day. There is undeniable character-building value in being self-reliant, but I'm worn out and weary. And I still have three more countries to go after this one.

9 BE MORE PIGLET

*'Piglet noticed that even though he had a Very Small Heart, it
could hold a rather large amount of Gratitude'*
– A. A. Milne

Driven by stubbornness, I ride just over 100 miles into a 18mph headwind to get out of Germany a day quicker. All day, Helga the Headwind – cruel and merciless tyrant that she is – does her best to crush my spirits. Towards the end of the day, after nine hours of riding without stopping, I am running on vapours. I didn't dare take a break all day because the wind had slowed my average speed down to a woeful range of 8–10mph and I knew I had a long way to go.

Rain pelts down and the wind violently whips around, causing the nearby trees to bend backwards as if they are made of flimsy yet supple rubber instead of sturdy wood. Their trunks don't seem at all designed to bend that far and I wonder how much more they can take before they break.

This is, without doubt, the worst weather of the trip so far, and in fact the worst weather I think I've ever cycled in; I couldn't have picked a worse day to ride a century with a loaded bike if I'd tried. No singing helps me today – I am quiet, tears occasionally rolling silently down my cheeks as I force myself to doggedly push on.

As always though, it is mind over matter and I deploy various mental tricks throughout the day. Switching off completely, quieting down my inner chatter and trying to focus on anything other than the discomfort I was feeling was key. At times, I try to pretend that I am actually completely separate to my own body and that I am in fact just witnessing someone else's suffering – I tell myself that it sucked to be that girl!

My knees are screaming at me by the time I eventually arrive into Husum, now just under 40 miles away from the Denmark border, desperate for food and trembling. It turns out that the only nearby restaurants are closed, the last-minute hotel I booked into has also stopped serving food and I'm cheerfully told by the receptionist that to go to the supermarket would require a mere 15 minute walk through town. It's 15 minutes I can't face – I'm well and truly defeated by the day. Dinner is my emergency can of rice pudding and the peanut butter wraps I didn't manage to eat during the day, washed down with the world's most expensive tiny bottle of orange juice from the mini bar in the room. I feel thankful for each and every mouthful and so entirely relieved to be off the road.

I soon pass out but later wake up in agony: my stomach cramps all night and I get intermittent chest burn. I assume it's due to lack of food but there's nothing I can do other than try not to think about the thousands of calories I've burned today versus the meagre few calories I've managed to replace. I feel horrendous, but I've also accidentally set a new benchmark for suffering and, despite my body screaming complaints at me, I'm filled with relief and pride to have made it through one of the toughest days on the bike I've ever known. This prompts another coping strategy that I use to survive the remaining six weeks on the road. I promise myself that no matter how bad things are, and how tough the day has been, at the end of every day, I will make a list of three things I am grateful for. I'm sure I could always find three things to be thankful for. This simple strategy has seen me through tough times before, and aching, exhausted and lonely, I cling to it now.

You may have come across the term stop-loss before; it relates to an action being taken (usually in investment or insurance) after a certain threshold is reached to prevent further damage – for example, shares are automatically sold when the value drops by a specified number of points in the stock market. In this way, the loss is stopped – it's a way of putting in some damage control. Humans protect their financial assets in this way but seem less inclined to apply it to their emotional resources. During endurance challenges, mindset is critical – I'd wager that more adventures end up failing due to state of mind rather anything else. Accordingly, I did my best to apply the stop-loss principle to my bad moods. I would give myself ten minutes or so a day, if needed, to really let off some steam – cry, rant or scream into the abyss if needed – but that was it. I don't think long-term complaining without action has ever really fixed a situation, but staying solution focused certainly has, and that was always what I tried to do. How can I make this better? If I can't change the circumstance, how can I change my attitude? Gratitude and power playlists are both extremely simple strategies but they've helped me through thousands of miles and countless hours of mental struggles, too. I've also learnt never to make an important decision when tired or hungry. Negative emotions are a bit like a toddler throwing a tantrum – it's not possible to ignore them completely but they shouldn't be in charge of making your important decisions for you.

'IT IS NOT ALLOWED. You must pay for that or eat it here.'

The next morning, I'm reminded of how very glad I am to be leaving Germany and its petty rules behind when I'm chastised by the waitress at the hotel breakfast buffet for the heinous crime of wrapping up a single mini bread roll in my napkin. I bite my lip and resist the urge to point out that if anyone is abusing the breakfast buffet, it's the family of American tourists that I've just seen go up for round number four, but instead I smile and smuggle the roll into my bike jersey pocket when she's not looking. Despite feeling worn out from yesterday's epic battle, this small interaction provides me with the motivation I need to hit the road. I've never been told off so many times in my adult life as I have in Germany, and all for things that really shouldn't matter. Good riddance to your rules, Germany!

I am once again battling against torrential rain and Helga's 20mph headwind all day but I focus on the progress I'm making, desperate to reach country number five. When I do at last reach the border for Denmark, I yelp with delight. I'm drenched to the core and weary, but not too tired to scream out with happiness at reaching another milestone. The rain is pelting down so violently it often stings but still I can't stop grinning like a Cheshire cat for the rest of the section.

DENMARK! Five countries down, three more to go. It feels incredible to be over the halfway mark of this huge journey and the simple act of crossing over the border provides a much needed morale boost. It seems that almost immediately the bike paths become smooth again. Oh, how I'd missed smooth tarmac and decent cycle infrastructure. I promise to never take simple things for granted ever again. My sense of humour also makes a welcome return and I cheerfully narrate the woeful weather situation to an imaginary audience, GoPro in hand: 'Well, at least I'm getting a free shower. Admittedly the water temperature could be a bit warmer.' Then, sticking my tongue out into the rain, 'Yep, definitely tastes Danish!'

That night, I finally manage to make a dent in the calorie deficit I'd accrued over the past few days and I devour the biggest plate of food I've ever seen: a gigantic breaded chicken fillet that came with an outrageous amount of potatoes and – the reason I selected it from the menu in the first place – a side jug of butter sauce, that as far as I can tell is just a jug of melted butter. I have a feeling I am going to like Denmark!

After making sure my plate is spotlessly clean, I then wolf down an apple crumble with ice cream. Food – simple, glorious, magnificent, wonderful food. Another thing I'd learnt not to take for granted. I muse on how much happier we would all be if we learnt to appreciate the little things, and then I begin to think through all of the many, many little things there are to appreciate. Food and shelter, firstly –even having these two fundamental things makes me a lot luckier than millions of people at that very same moment.

Forcing myself to remember that, the challenges of the day are put into perspective.

The next day, signs of sheer exhaustion are growing ever more prominent. I've got some early symptoms of a urinary tract infection, which makes for a very uncomfortable day, and I catch myself unintentionally weaving across the road a few times due to extreme tiredness. Thankfully, Danish cycle paths keep me largely separate from the traffic, but this is no way to ride.

It becomes even more obvious that I'm not in the best state when, despite weeks of cycling in Europe, I forget to look left when crossing over the road and cause both me and a driver to slam on our brakes, narrowly missing what would have been a horrible collision. I prepare myself for a barrage of abuse from the driver but find that he is more concerned about my safety than angry at my stupidity. I apologise profusely and I feel very glad to have a rest day lined up for the next day. Legs angrily twinging and internal battery levels utterly drained, I feel like the cycling dead. I am run down to the point of breaking and desperate to rest. I'm at my limit. I go to a cash point, eagerly anticipating the feast I can buy for dinner.

That night, after checking in to the friendly hostel for my weekly rest day, I am devastated to realise that I have once again managed to time my booking with the one day (Sunday) they are not serving any food . . . and the nearest restaurant is a one mile walk away. It's a struggle to stay awake long enough at the restaurant table to eat my food and when I leave in a daze, I don't remember to take my wallet with me after paying – a fact I won't realise until the next morning when I head to the supermarket in the next town to do my usual rest day supermarket sweep.

Accordingly, my one sacred weekly rest day becomes a

frantic series of overtired, irrational and very teary phone calls with Mum as I berate myself for being such an idiot. I retrace the walking route to the restaurant, scanning the grassy side of the road to no avail and then reach the restaurant to discover they are only open Friday to Sunday, Today is Monday, so there is no one there whom I can ask about my wallet. I wonder what to do with the fact that I'm in the middle of Denmark with no money, not least of all without a way to pay for the hostel I'm currently staying in.

However, it turns out that the lovely hostel manager – who never falters in his hospitality despite both of our growing concerns that I might not be able to actually pay him – thankfully knows the owner of the restaurant, Elspeth, and says he will try to call her so she can check the restaurant. Thanking my previous self for having the sense to go to the cash point and *not* put all of my cash in my wallet, I ride the four-miles to the supermarket where I spend frugally. I'll be eating instant noodles and bread with peanut butter for the rest of the day, for every meal, and for breakfast the next morning.

When I get back to the hostel, I'm told that Elsbeth will be unable to check the restaurant until 8:30am the next day, so I'm in for another day of waiting whilst praying the restaurant has my wallet. Despite the stormy panic that rages around my body, I fall asleep in the afternoon and wake up only to eat before crashing out again. Exhaustion is clearly taking its toll.

By now, the perhaps slightly over ambitious schedule I wrote out for myself before leaving has become both law and comforter to me – I dare not deviate, add an extra rest day or ever adjust the mileage. In hindsight, I definitely didn't factor in enough rest time. The longest adventure I'd done before was four weeks in total, and I am finding out the hard way that naively pushing things at the same pace on a much longer trip is a recipe for suffering. I have been on the road for 6 weeks and I have ridden over 2,000 miles so far - and my body is simply unable to recover at the rate I am wearing it out.

Follow a schedule no matter what perhaps doesn't sound particularly adventurous, but I did find it helpful to have a target to aim for. Importantly for me, it was also one less choice to make and one less thing to work out – when I am emotionally and mentally drained from all the hundreds of smaller decisions I have to make every single day, anything that simplifies things at this stage becomes vital.

Decision fatigue, muscle fatigue, emotional fatigue, too much peanut butter fatigue – if it had been some weird game of Fatigue Bingo, I would have had a full house. In addition, I'd also based my speaking dates back home on this schedule – it is the scaffolding around which everything else is built. The thought of having to now throw it all into chaos to collect money because I was silly enough to leave my wallet behind causes tears to bubble just under the surface. It's not at all rational but weariness is building up and I find myself more and more emotionally akin to a toddler, the slightest mishap liable to set off a tantrum.

The next morning, I ride the unloaded bike to the restaurant, wondering if I'll soon be taking a detour of hundreds of miles to the nearest Western Union in Copenhagen to collect emergency money wired over by Mum. I'm on the verge of tears when I reach it, my heart pounding loudly in my chest as I see Elsbeth walk to the door . . . waving my wallet in her hand! Without hesitation or restraint of any kind, I rush straight over and envelop Elsbeth – who I have only just met and haven't even spoken to yet – in a gigantic hug. Luckily, Elspeth doesn't mind the friendly tackle and shares my unbridled joy at having found the wallet – saying through her laughter that she is happy that I am happy. I do a little happy dance, which she does not join me in, but she does supportively clap along. I vow to not complain about anything for the rest of the day. And I also vow to be more careful. So far, Denmark has shown me nothing but kindness in response to my idiocy, and for that I am immensely grateful.

The ride to Thyborøn is stunning, with bright blue skies and endless views. After days spent rolling alongside grey buildings and traffic, it's nourishing to be reunited with the coast again and I feel renewed by the fresh sea air and gorgeous views. For every moment of tiredness on a long trip, there are hundreds more filled with simple content-ment and peace.

Later that day, as I walk along the main road to the supermarket, a car stops and someone shouts something out at me. I assume it's because although there is no footpath and there's no other place I could possibly be walking, I'm not walking against the direction of traffic and he is telling me off. Upon realising that I don't speak Danish he explains in English that he is actually offering me a lift! I love Denmark.

Nonetheless, a deep level of tiredness that just can't be fixed with one rest day a week is now starting to set in. In the midst of a record-breaking heatwave that is causing issues for farmers across Europe, the days often feel long, cruel and punishing. Mark Kleanthous emails me some encouragement and I take to repeating his suggested mantra 'Laura is invincible' to myself. Each and every day is now a battle to ignore how tired I am and I realise that now, more than ever, my attitude matters. Each and every day, I continue to make myself find things to be grateful for. I remind myself of all the miserable hours I'd wasted in various jobs and this nearly always helps to makes me feel better. When that doesn't quite cut it and I find myself longing for air-conditioning, I imagine a formidable thought ninja by my side, fly kicking away all negative thoughts with a dramatic 'HIIIIIII-YA' that would make Bruce Lee proud.

During my next rest day, in Hantsholm, I have a Skype interview with *Cooler* magazine which reminds me to appreciate the uniqueness of what I'm doing and, in recapping my story, how far I've come since my unfulfilling days in an office. When I'm asked how I feel about the impending end of the trip, I'm also reminded to savour life on the road and that this will soon be all over. Although I am desperate to finish, I also feel my first pang of sadness that I will soon be leaving it all behind.

A slight niggle in my right leg continues to angrily flare up, and is only temporarily relieved by stretching it out during snack breaks. My body is slowly but surely breaking down. Whatever adaptations I felt weeks ago seem to have plateaued, and I feel myself getting ever more tired, ever more depleted, and it's all I can do to just keep going. I hope that whatever little I have left is enough to get me to Bergen.

On my penultimate day in Denmark, the pressure valve bursts and I find myself sobbing next to a picnic bench on the side of the road. Tears of frustration, tears of exhaustion and tears of simply having had enough. Torturing myself with the thoughts of all my friends enjoying this glorious summer – all the barbecues, outdoor swimming and park picnics I'm missing out on – I daydream about quitting. I run through all the different ways I could quit – and it's bliss. I get lost for hours thinking of how wonderful it would feel to just pack it all in and to not have to endure this sufferfest for a moment longer. Ultimately, I know I won't give up but the thought alone provides such relief.

The relentless headwind and unfaltering heat continues to bear down and I am mindful of rationing water each day. Whenever I catch a reflection of myself, I see bloodshot eyes wearily staring back at me. Picture perfect scenery that I know I'm not always fully appreciating rolls by, but I want nothing more than to rest. As I creep ever closer to country number seven, Sweden, the landscape finally begins to undulate once more. After cycling endlessly long and flat roads for weeks, I am surprisingly overjoyed to see the hills. They target different muscle groups in my legs, allowing some groups to recover whilst others work, as opposed to the constant strain of flat riding and incessant pedalling, usually against the wind. Most importantly, I get to enjoy some downhill coasting – a luxury I have not had since leaving the UK!

I reach country number seven courtesy of ferry number twenty. At long last, with my thirty-second birthday happening the next day, I have scheduled two (two!!) days off in a row for the first time since this journey began nearly two months ago. On the ferry to Varberg, I eat three full platefuls of food from the buffet before the ship has even started to move, and I then move to the outside upper deck and find myself a bench in the shade, where I promptly fall asleep. I momentarily wake up to get an ice cream and then fall asleep again.

As a birthday treat, my mum has booked me into a luxury hotel – for the next 48 hours I am in power saving mode. When my brother Rhys calls to wish me happy birthday, I admit that I'm starting to feel a bit worn down and I'm starting to miss home – it feels strange to be completely alone on my birthday. He manages to make me laugh and cheerfully reminds me that they've all been checking in on me regularly via my tracker map. I smile to think of my nieces and nephews watching my progress on a screen, following my mini-me as it draws a red line across the map – where is Auntie Laura today?

Making sure to savour every minute in my lavish surroundings, I rise from the gigantic bed only to eat or to slowly meander over to the in-house spa, where, after lazily splashing around in all three ornate pools, I'm treated to an overly oily and amusingly gentle massage, that does nothing for my now severely knotted muscles. At all other times, I am asleep. When it is time to leave, I consider boarding up the expensive hotel doors and refusing to leave.

For the first two hours on the road to Gothenburg, my legs are heavy and reluctant. This is a brutal cycle I'm beginning to know well – never quite recovering on my token weekly rest days, often just breaking the rhythm and feeling all out of sorts when it's time to move again. This time, however, the extra day seems to have done wonders and my legs settle down earlier than usual. All the same, it's 8pm when I fall asleep and, when I wake up 11 hours later at 7am, I am drenched in sweat, having broken a fever during the night, my body desperately trying to repair the muscles fast enough to keep up with my ruthless demands.

When I check in with Mum and tell her of my exhaustion, she quite reasonably responds to my struggles by suggesting I get the ferry directly to Stavanger – missing out the last three days of the trip. Only, this isn't at all logical to me, and I completely lose my temper. 'I didn't come all this way to cheat,' I snap at her. It angers me that she's trying to figure out a shortcut rather than supporting me and believing in me to do the challenge I set out to. Which of course, is not at all what's happening here. Somewhere, I know she's trying to help but, irrational and exhausted, my temper is on a short fuse. Fully engrossed in my selfish self-pity party, I tell her it's hard enough without her seeds of doubt being planted. Why can't she just encourage me to carry on, rather than pander to my complaints of being tired and run down? It's unfair of me – it's of course totally natural that her maternal instinct would react to my suffering and want to somehow lessen it. But there is no logic to be found at that moment. Feeling terrible at having unintentionally caused me further distress, even though she is clearly not at fault, she sends me a lovely message wishing me a good day.

The terrain is now undoubtedly hilly again. I use my full range of gears for the first time since leaving the UK. All day, I think of how much I'm struggling and I think of the infamously rugged terrain of Norway still to come. Mum's well-intended suggestion is still lingering, and the gremlin pounces: if this is hard, how will I do what is still to come? I managed Scotland, I remind myself, but that seems like a long time ago now – my energy was fresher. Arguably, my legs are now stronger but I don't know which is more relevant to being able to succeed at this any more. I just feel totally done in and intimidated by all the miles I have yet to cover. I expected to feel at my strongest by this point in the ride but I just feel worn down and paper thin. I feel like I'm getting weaker. I focus on all that is to be gained by perse-vering and all that is to be lost if I give up now. Most impor-tantly, I focus on all the promise I made to myself before leaving – to go all in. That finish line is so close, I remind myself. Just one final push.

A gravel section forces me off the bike and the relentless heat burns. More hills. I am travelling just slow enough for the flies to swarm around me – no doubt attracted by the litres of sweat pouring off me. Eventually, I break through the rut and the views help me smile again. Nonetheless, I feel like a hollowed out shell of the woman I was when I began in Scotland, with only glimpses of the inner spark that drove me to take this challenge on in the first place. I tell myself that where there is even a small spark, there is hope; I cling to that ember and try to trust that it's enough to keep me going.

All day I think of how much I miss my family and friends; all the things I'd rather be doing (mostly sleeping). Despite this, when Mum calls to make amends that night, I can't bring myself to speak to her. I'm still sulking like a spoilt teenager and, having just stopped for the day, I have no energy for interaction of any kind: the thought of an evening debrief is too much. The bad temper fuses with the guilt of being a horrible daughter. I am hurting and lashing out – it's not fair and it's not behaviour I'm proud of.

The monumentally beautiful views stop me in my tracks a couple of times, always near water, but generally I have to admit that the novelty seems to have worn off. I look back at photos and surprise myself with how lovely the views are. In a state of constant tiredness, apparently I appreciate them more in hindsight.

The next day, I cross over the border I've been working towards for 58 days. Country number eight – the final one: Norway. When I cross over the bridge that separates Sweden and Norway, I accidentally zoom straight past the sign without realising. I then go back to get a photo. I've been thinking all day, and for all the days beforehand, how it might feel to cross into the final country – I thought I'd feel a surge of emotions, maybe even cry out in dramatic elation or perhaps have a little celebratory wiggle along to a power anthem! Instead, I take a quiet moment – but only a moment – and then carry on pedalling. This journey is not over yet.

It's once again ridiculously hot and, as if setting the tone for the days that follow, I am immediately faced with a huge hill minutes after crossing the border – a very fitting welcome to the country. My quiet satisfaction at having reached the milestone of Norway is somewhat dampened by the knowledge that there is still so much fighting to be done and I'm weary.

The next day leads me to believe that if Norwegian weather was a person, they would suffer from multiple personality disorder and would undoubtedly be a perfect match for the similarly afflicted Scottish weather. After eating some instant noodles for breakfast, I head out, only to be immediately faced with the wrath of Helga, who is apparently feeling particularly vicious. I was once told of the Scandinavian saying that 'The north wind made the Vikings'. This sometimes spurs me on, and I daydream about channelling the spirit of a formidable and fierce Viking warrior against the elements – but, in my more cynical moments, I bet that even the stout-hearted Vikings wished that the wind would just give it a rest sometimes. As I wearily fight for every inch of progress, I once again toy with the idea of quitting. Then it rains, a situation I take very personally.

Eventually, I make it to yet another ferry and I'm delighted to discover that, though it's only small, this one serves hot food. To celebrate, I treat myself to chicken and rice and wash it all down with a chocolate milkshake. I disembark the ferry to find hot sunshine, less wind and, having bumped up my calories, I'm also in a much better mood. I push on, motivated by yet another cheap bed to sleep in tonight.

When I do finally arrive at the hostel, I am horrified to discover that all of the nearby cafés and restaurants are again all closed. I liberate Dory from her panniers and together we set off to ride the 30 minutes to the nearest supermarket, but then lightning cracks, thunder roars and a violent downpour follows. I consider going anyway when I see a steep descent I'll have to go down . . . which naturally means a very steep ascent on the way back. It's the final hurdle I don't have it in me to face – I turn back and accept dinner tonight will be a tin of mackerel, a leftover peanut butter wrap and a couple of cereal bars. I discover half a cucumber – which, after being exposed to 32 degree heat and sweating in its plastic wrapper all day had definitely seen better days, but I cover it in peanut butter and eat it anyway. All in all, not too bad for an improvised picnic! I have two stale wraps leftover for breakfast and make a mental note to raid the supermarket tomorrow.

Dad, now back home and much better, calls as I'm preparing my makeshift dinner. I don't mean to burst into tears when I answer, but unexpectedly they just erupt out of me – it surprises both of us. I share the story of my woeful dinner. Miraculously, he manages to somehow take me from tears to laughter almost immediately. His usual 'I remember when I was on Everest . . .' fairytale begins. I've heard several versions of this elaborate and totally made up story throughout my life – the key ingredients being a huge physical feat combined with completely impractical and ridiculous odds. Previous versions have started with 'I remember when I was in a rowing boat in the Pacific, with only toothpicks for oars!'. Tonight, he follows up his fabricated and absurd mountaineering tale with, 'And I only had a tin of mackerel – between six of us! Count yourself lucky.' He then adds, 'Name them. It'll make them last longer if you thank each and every one before you eat them.'

I have to hand it to my Dad – he can nearly always make me laugh, no matter how dire the situation. Everything seems a little brighter and a lot more doable after a little laughter. He goes on to tell me how proud he is, how not many people could have gotten this far and how he couldn't have done it. Emerging from my mega sulk, I think of my poor Mum, who has been frequently faced with the raw, irrational and grumpy creature – akin to a bear woken too early from hibernation – I have come to resemble recently. Mum, being an internationally respected and highly admired life coach, was generally one for taking my complaints more seriously and empathising, as we strategically worked through whatever might be going on. Both approaches had strengths. Usually offloading to Mum makes me feel better, and Dad's insistence of humour in the face of my terribly serious suffering could sometimes make me feel infuriated. But tonight, Dad's terrible jokes have made me feel better – they've lightened my spirits and a dose of laughter was just what I needed.

I call Mum to apologise for being so unfairly ill-tempered with her and I then go through the last section of the route, cleaning things up a bit. I'd gotten lazy with my planning when I got to this section and, I was now realising, I'd also been really over ambitious. My blasé assumption that I'd be strong enough to just get on with it by now was great in theory, but after weeks of flat terrain, the elevation of Norway means I'm burning way more calories and my tired muscles are screaming. I'm near the finish, but I'm not near enough to be reckless just yet. I still need to manage things.

The legendary terrain of Norway lives up to every bold

and leg-twitch-inducing story I've ever heard – climb, after climb, after climb. I settle into my pain cave as I drag Dory and I ever upwards. So. Many. Hills! They seem to turn corners and go on forever. The hairpin descents are often terrifying – my brakes feel feeble against the gravity of a steep drop and heavily loaded bike. I mutter 'Keep us safe, Dory' throughout the day, nervously pleading with her to look after me as she always has done.

On one morning, I lose it, shouting out 'This is impossible!' to the empty road. Within 30 minutes of every day, I am always drenched in sweat. The phenomenal heat and the formidable hills are breaking me. Desperately, I regularly tumble into various petrol stations where I devour, as a minimum, an iced tea, an iced coffee and a toasted panini. I usually stop again an hour later for another chilled coffee and, of course, an Orange Fanta. The terrain stays hot and hilly but with the help of petrol stations, I manage to keep going. If nothing else, I remind myself that I can at least appreciate the views.

The breathtaking views are frequently interrupted by the tunnels that cut through the mountains – although I initially savour the cooler temperature of these tunnels, the amplified roar of the traffic is phenomenal and intimidating. I repeatedly cringe at the thought of how many accidents must happen in tunnels just like these. Before going in to each one, I make sure to turn on all of my bike lights and then, for added measure, I sing loudly for the entire duration until I reach the other side. By the third tunnel, I have in fact written my own bespoke tunnel song – the lyrics being both simple and immensely practical:

'Please don't squish me, I'm too young to die.

Please don't squish me, give me lots of room and safely drive on by.'

Although I sing my somewhat morbid ditty at full volume through each and every tunnel, I needn't have been so worried – Norwegian drivers seem to be the most considerate of the whole trip. All day, they are patient and give me plenty of room.

My next rest day takes place in the beautiful town of Arendal. There are now only two weeks left on the road; I've never been closer to Bergen but I'm feeling destroyed. Earlier that year, I'd become an ambassador for Power Traveller, and as part of our partnership they'd supplied me a solar charger, that I can lay across my panniers, and a rechargeable battery bank. This outrageous heat wave meant that I'd never struggled to keep my gear charged, even if the same could not be said for my own energy levels. In a final attempt to lighten the load, I post back my second and unused battery bank with lots of help from the very friendly staff at the local post office. I then take Dory in to the very friendly local bike shop, who kindly adjust her brakes, and I spend the rest of the day hanging out with Oliver, the very friendly dog who belongs to the very friendly B&B owner, Izzie.

The next day, of course, I get a very friendly send off. It is the B&B's second anniversary so at breakfast there is a gigantic and elaborately decorated cake sat amidst the breakfast buffet. Izzie insist that I have some cake with my 8am breakfast, as not only is it the perfect fuel for climbing the mountains ahead, we also have to celebrate! Who am I to argue? Some might say *carpe diem* – I say carpe cake-um. I leave full of energy, following two cups of coffee and two slices of cake, in addition to two rounds of scrambled egg on bread.

'Are you ready for the mountains?' Izzie asks, as I hand over the keys to yesterday's home.

'I am now!' I cheerfully reply, sugar and caffeine coursing rapidly through my veins.

She tells me she is very impressed and wishes me all the best for my trip, telling me it will be beautiful ahead. I don't doubt it – for all of Norway's challenges, it's breathtakingly stunning.

In a caring, maternal voice she adds 'Drive safe', after hugging me goodbye. I leave Arendal stocked up on good-will – and reminded of just how much I have missed simple human connection.

The kindness of Arendal sees me through a hideous gravel section that follows soon after leaving. I am forced to walk the bike for just under an hour through a forest; flies and various other biting insects swarm around and dive at me. It is frustrating on the flat sections but completely absurd on the hills – it is all I can do to keep me and Dory upright, my feet sliding and the tires slipping. When the forest does clear, however, it reveals a view that renders me speechless – a lake stretches out into the distance, the sunlight glimmering on the water and the steep terrain towering above it on both sides. All the same, it is a huge relief when we find ourselves back on tarmac.

The next morning, I look in the mirror of a petrol station bathroom and shudder at my run-down appearance – there are bags under my bloodshot eyes and my usually clear complexion is peppered in spots. Shortly after, I'm feeling extremely sorry for myself when a friendly cyclist joins me for five minutes of chat uphill, which provides a welcome morale boost. He had said something in Norwegian to which I replied, 'I'm sorry, I'm English, I don't understand.' But, as with most people in Norway, he speaks perfect English. He questions me about the route I've already taken and the route I will continue to take, telling me that I have a lot to look forward to – including some very big mountains! He commends me on my challenge before speeding off towards Mandel – where I am also headed, albeit much slower. Before disappearing into the distance, he advises me there is great coffee and cake in Mandel so I also have that to look forward to. I soon find myself alone again and the next two hours on the road seem to drag forever. After only one hour I stop at a petrol station and get a Snickers ice cream, but even that doesn't seem to pick me up.

Thirty minutes later, I find myself sat in bus stop shelter, desperately trying to summon some of the energy I need to continue. It's just so unbearably hot. I sit on the bench with my head in my hands feeling burnt out. Fortunately, a wasp comes angrily buzzing and breaks me out of the rut, reminding me it is time to move.

The next time I stop at a petrol station it is three hours later and it's in desperation. I wolf down a baguette, a mango iced tea, an Orange Fanta and another bottle of water. For the first time all day, I feel myself coming to life. Which is just as well because moments later I find myself battling another gravel section – this time having to not only walk the bike up the hill but also having to walk it down the hill because the slippery gravel makes it too risky to ride. Down we slowly walk, with me tightly squeezing the brakes in an attempt to maintain some tentative control. I consider that I've unintentionally created a new sport and decide to call it bike-hiking – I almost immediately conclude that this is actually a terrible sport and it will never catch on. I lose the best part of an hour bike-hiking.

Back onto the busy roads, I am greeted once more with the trifecta of misery: headwind, heat and more hills. The longest hill of the day takes an hour of non-stop climbing to reach the top – I am completely drenched in sweat, fat droplets of it falling onto the road and handlebars. With a loaded bike, this is brutal. Once again, pushed to the brink, I feel victorious in my exhaustion. The rest of the route is downhill from here. This is a thought that would normally fill me with joy, however the descents are terrifying – steep with corners that turn sharply. I find myself once again firmly squeezing the brakes and saying a silent prayer to the universe and a not so silent request to Dory – please keep us safe. Thankfully, the views make up for it and I think if I am to suffer, I'm glad it's somewhere as beautiful as Norway.

It's a busy Saturday, and when I do make it back down from the mountains and approach the cities, the roads are full of traffic. The drivers are still respectful but the constant noise and extra attention needed only exacerbates my weariness. Just when I feel ready to fall out with the day, I turn a corner and arrive at the most gorgeous beach. First things first, it is time for a swim. I feel the stresses of the day melt away in an instant as I lazily float in the cool water of the fjord and look out to the nearby mountains. This is the best reward I could have ever imagined. All at once, the day is one of my favourites. Magical, sneaky Norway, often taking me to breaking point and then suddenly making it all so much better than I ever could have dreamt it to be.

The next morning, my body once again feels like it's been filled with lead overnight. I'd purposely thrown in a lower mileage day to try and recover so there is only 25 miles scheduled for today, but I know better than to be complacent, having learnt over time on the road that anything can happen. In fact, it usually happens on the days that should be easier. This day is no exception; the route to

Flekkefjord goes down as my least favourite of the entire trip.

I quickly find myself on a gravel section which, as per usual, I have to walk. Eventually finding my way back to tarmac, the relief is short lived when I'm greeted with a 'no cycling' sign. The Komoot app, which up until now I've been using to successfully navigate for thousands of miles, is seemingly oblivious to the fact that the route it intends me to take is in fact illegal. I navigate my way around the first of these signs, taking a seven-mile detour. I soon find myself faced with another one and a rotten decision to make – obeying the signs would mean doubling my distance for the day, an unbearable thought which seems completely pointless and unbelievably cruel in this steep terrain. I decide to take my chances, reasoning that even if the roads are busy, I won't be on them for that long, and it has to be better than adding another five hours to my day.

As choices go, this turns out to be a terrible one and I soon understood all too well why bicycles aren't allowed. I find myself in yet more tunnels, these ones much bigger and busier than previous editions; the drivers travelling significantly faster and the margin of room for me and Dory significantly smaller. Unlike yesterday's intimidating but ultimately harmless tunnels, these are inarguably terrifying. By the time I reach them, however, it is too late to turn back and there is no other route to take. I have no option but to carry on – I can't get to the other side of the dual carriageway even if I wanted to.

Each and every tunnel is a horrible, frenzied experience as Dory and I cling desperately to the tiny side ledges – unable to ride for fear of accidentally brushing up against the traffic, I'm carefully walking us through. With no other viable alternative, I carry on – tunnel after tunnel – cursing my decision to cut out the extra miles. The final tunnel of the day has less of a side ledge and more of a side sand pit. I trip over a hidden circle of wire buried just under the sand and go flying forwards, desperately trying to control my fall as I go so that I don't move even an inch to the left, where the traffic is hurtling past at 70mph. Briefly unleashing verbal fury on the wire, I dust myself down and keep moving. This is no place to linger – the tantrum will have to wait.

Traffic thunders past, lorries passing so close as to hit me with waves of wind as they go. Occasionally, horns angrily beep at me in a symphony when any cautious drivers slow down in order to pass. This only makes me angrier – I know they're right and this was a bad idea. Internally, I'm shouting out in response that I think we can all agree that this was a terrible decision and I have clearly made a huge error in judgement but it's not like I have any way of getting out of it now, so can everyone PLEASE STOP BEEPING. Externally, I remain focussed on just getting to the other side without incident. 'The light at the end of the tunnel' takes on a whole new meaning for me today.

Despite there being one near miss in the tunnels of doom (not their actual name), the worst point of the day actually takes place in bright daylight, just as I think the worst is over. A lorry goes to overtake me, but when a car comes around the corner in the opposite direction, the lorry quickly moves back over, forcing me to slam my brakes on and smash myself into a nearby rock wall to avoid getting squished. It misses me by inches and then carries on, apparently oblivious. I don't think I've ever had such a close call in my entire life – I really hope I don't ever have one again. I'm shaken up when I finish for the day, feeling a renewed sense of gratitude for simply being alive. There were too many close calls to count and I vow to never be so stupid again.

Once again diving into a nearby lake before tackling dinner, I lie motionless in the water and imagine the stress of the day washing away. It's partly successful but I could really do with a hug. Craving human company, I choose to treat myself to a hostel room. However, this becomes another decision I regret when it turns out that the other residents of the hostel, a group of Germans, insist on playing horrendous Europop/dance music at full volume whilst getting ever more drunk and rowdy. It's such a serene setting – completely at odds with the obnoxious behaviour of the group. When I bump into one of them in the communal kitchen, mascara smeared down her face, she has a cigarette dangling from one hand and is waving a bottle of Jack Daniels around in the other – alcohol literally sweating out through her pores, combining with a stench of stale sweat that makes me gag. Which in itself is actually quite impressive because I'm used to being the smelliest person in most rooms on this trip, but I'm absolutely sure that not even my sweat and dirt infused lycra smelt that bad.

If there is one bonus to being at the hostel it is that there are ice packs in the communal kitchen freezer. I take two of them and place one on each of my legs as I cram mouthfuls of rice into my mouth. All night, my neighbours continue to do absolutely everything at an antisocial volume. I try to be zen about the situation, thinking that a bigger person would show compassion, perhaps wishing her fellow humans peace and happiness. Instead I constantly fantasise about telling them to shut up but instead I just lie there and angrily stew, literally, in the hot room. My legs burn and I am feverish; yet again I struggle to sleep in the heat. All night and into the early hours of the morning, I hear the group creaking around – like oversized and vastly overfed rats.

I make myself feel infinitely better when I think how much I will enjoy making a lot of noise very early in the morning, when no doubt they will be very hungover. Zen compassion – o, petty (but oh so satisfying) revenge – 1.

After a hectic start the next day, I soon find myself on blissfully quiet roads. The views are absolutely incredible and often stop me in my tracks – I can't believe what I'm seeing. Huge fjords, mountains and quiet roads all to myself – I'm 90 per cent sure that these are the most beautiful roads I have ever seen.

'OK, Norway, I forgive you for yesterday,' I say under my breath.

Soon enough, I find myself pushing the bike up slippery gravel in a forest again, but it's hard to stay mad when the views are so magical. Then I'm back onto tarmac and the views continue to keep me happily distracted. However, the idyllic morning lulls me into a false sense of security. I have no way of knowing that what lies ahead is the worst condition of road – road in the very loosest sense of the word – I have ever seen.

I am forced to walk with the bike again, both of us slipping all over the ever-shifting surface. I can't work out if it is gravelly sand or sandy gravel and I wonder what ratios would determine it either way. I try to ride it occasionally but find that we slip even more. On I go, pushing the bike in 29 degree heat with flies swarming, horseflies biting, wasps buzzing, sweat pouring. Onwards I push, expecting that soon enough I would find tarmac as I always do.

Two and a half hours later I am still pushing the bike. All sense of humour is now long gone. In contrast to yesterday's heaving traffic, today I've barely seen two cars in as many hours. I was relying on seeing at least one petrol station, but of course there are none. Now my water is running low and I am dehydrated from what feels like litres of sweat loss. Head pounding, lungs heaving and legs burning, I am feeling ruined. With 12 miles left to go, I wonder how long that will take to walk in this state – it's a bleak thought but one I think I have to accept because these precarious roads are impossible to ride. The tantalisingly clear fjord lies hundreds of metres below and I'm running out of water. Onwards, slowly crawling forwards.

'F**k you, Norway,' I mutter under my breath. So fickle, considering that nearly hours earlier I was confessing my undying love. But that was then and now I am tired, thirsty, hungry, totally over it all and I just want to be done.

Thankfully, after yet more bike-hiking, the last eight miles are on tarmac. Although these final eight miles still feature a lot of climbing, at least I'm able to cycle in, rather than struggling to push a fully loaded bike on constantly changing terrain.

Getting increasingly desperate, I use my MSR water filter in the first source of water I come across in hours – a small lake, well . . . more of a glorified large puddle. Dead flies float on the surface and the stagnant water looks revolting, but I have no other options. I fill up an 'emergency' bottle that I hope I won't need to touch and I further ration the little amount of non-puddle water that I have left; my throat feels dry and scratchy and my head hurts. I wobble all over the road, feeling at my very limit.

'Just keep going, just a little further,' I tell myself. I don't have the energy to sing along to my playlist but I listen to it anyway and think of the people that recommended songs.

Each one of them I now imagine cheering me on from the sidelines as I slowly and stubbornly push forwards.

At last, I see a petrol station with only 1.5 miles to go. Normally being so close to the finish point of the day I'd wait but I am truly desperate. Two milkshakes (both strawberry), one mango iced tea, one bottle of water and a Snickers ice cream bar – all devoured immediately. I don't think I've ever been so thirsty.

Dinner that night is eaten at a nearby hostel once again – it is a stew, an unappealing grey slop with mashed potato. My heart sinks at the dismal sight of it . . . until I take my first bite. It is, without doubt, the best slop I've ever tasted. I devour three full platefuls and each one tastes delicious because I'm so depleted. Much to my eternal gratitude, my mum had sneakily upgraded my booking so instead of a cheap shared hostel room, I find myself sleeping in an idyllic cabin for the night! Complete with kitchen, comfy sofa and hot shower – that beautiful cabin has everything I could ever want.

I shut the door and immediately collapse onto the sofa, exhausted but strangely exhilarated after a day of battling the Norwegian terrain. I feel proud for overcoming it all – that in itself is energising. For the first time in days – if not weeks – I look in the mirror after rinsing the encrusted dirt and sweat away and I see a spark in my eye I haven't seen for ages. I feel strong for achieving today. I feel like even though Norway has tried to defeat me for the second day in a row, I am not going down without a fight. I fall asleep listening to the soothing sounds of a nearby brook bubbling away.

Stocking up the next morning at the local supermarket, I am greeted by a very affectionate cat who wraps herself around me as I reload the bike. The effects of loneliness now clearly apparent, I spend ten minutes with my new furry friend and briefly consider taking her with me, before then shuddering at the thought of carrying any extra weight up into the mountains. I give her one last cuddle and say goodbye.

I am on the road for a mere 15 minutes before I am once again saturated in sweat. Greeted immediately by a steep hill, I accept defeat and begin to push, rather than attempt to ride, the bike up the sharp ascent. Progress is an excruciatingly slow 2mph; every muscle in my body is aching. The only real motivation to keep moving comes from the flies swarming again around my head, occasionally diving directly into my eyes.

I manage to travel at a slightly speedier 7mph when my legs warm up enough and remember how to climb hills, but I'm devoid of any kind of vitality today. It's all I can do to keep moving. The heat is suffocating and I'm not travelling anywhere near fast enough to get a breeze. I brace myself for a day of torment but, after a morning of suffering, my luck turns and all of my climbing is rewarded – it is downhill for the rest of the day! Right then I consider that if I could somehow wrap my arms around a country and hug Norway, I would.

The next day, I am headed to Stavanger. It's beautiful and scenic to start. I am falling a bit more in love with this country every day. Within minutes on the road, a friendly cyclist chats to me as he passes – he has just spent four weeks cycling around Norway. Amidst so many hours with only my own thoughts for company, small, simple and seemingly insignificant interactions like this one make my day.

In no mood for novelty detours or gravelly paths, I decide to stick to the busy main roads, even though, with them, comes the compromise of noise and stress. I stop at a petrol station and get chatting to two more friendly local cyclists, who seem concerned that I am following the busy E39 road when there are much more peaceful options available. We spend ten minutes with maps discussing all the alternative routes. I consider following their advice and heading to the coast once more until one of them says, 'It's a bit longer but it's much more beautiful.' I don't say anything but I know he has lost me at 'it's a bit longer'.

We chat some more – one says how he went touring for three days with his bike and remarking that 'It is good for my shape – the bike is so heavy.' He asks if I have noticed a difference in my body shape. I laugh, ice cream in hand, and joke that there is little difference because I eat so much ice cream. It is a pleasure to chat to them; one of them then gently asks, 'You must be tired after being on the road for two months, are you ready to go home?' I confess that I am ready for a rest and he nods in sympathy. I love Norway. I muse again later that it is human contact that makes touring – and indeed life – so special and now I am having more conversations, I am enjoying things much more again.

The rest of the day features noisy lorries and busy traffic until I near Stavanger, when bike paths start to reappear. With only an hour left to go I stop at a petrol station, intending only to buy a few small snacks. Instead, I somehow find myself in the takeaway pizza restaurant next door where I accidentally order a medium pizza when I go to pay for my can of trusty Orange Fanta. Thankfully, I visit the toilet before attempting to eat anything, because the rather robust lorry driver that was in there before me was clearly experiencing digestion issues – the overwhelming smell hits me in the back of my throat as soon as I go in and it repeatedly makes me gag. I desperately need to pee so I bury my nose into the smelly armpit of my cycling jersey to mask the smell and avoid vomiting. Thankfully, this works, and by comparison to the unholy aroma in the toilet my stale jersey smells like a bouquet of flowers. It's a huge relief when I am then once again surrounded by the comforting smell of pizza when I head back to wait for my impromptu meal.

I head back outside and wolf down the pizza in the car park by the bins. Adventure is nothing if not glamorous! As soon as I hit my first post-pizza hill, though, I instantly regret my food choice. I am so full and the unnecessary extra garlic sauce that I added on a whim to the pizza is now getting burped back up again. Impulse control is clearly not my strong point today.

At last, I reach Stavanger. From here, I could take a final ferry all the way to Bergen if I wanted. This was the ferry option that had so enraged me when Mum had suggested it days ago. It was now within such easy grasp – I could be finished! The temptation is almost overpowering; I have never felt so exhausted in my entire life. Although I know that I am tantalisingly close to the finish, it still feels so far. Body, mind and spirit are all worn out – I am tired in my bones. But I force myself to think of all the miles I have done so far. I remind myself that I have done too many to take a shortcut now. Instead I opt for a final rest day in Stavanger. I have just three days left – even if I have to go slowly, I can't quit now.

As has become customary on my one rest day a week, I sleep and eat – without doing much else in between. As I restock supplies for the final push in the local supermarket, my weary spirits are warmed by the fact that everyone is so friendly. There is no doubt at all that I've fallen in love with Norway and could easily live here – the wilderness, the beauty, the culture have all etched a permanent place for themselves in my heart. But, I'm also really ready to come home. I'm restless – feeling like I'm stuck in limbo out here whilst the lives of everyone I care about back home continues to zoom along without me. I'm ready for life to un-pause.

It's a groggy start the next morning. Always the same after a rest – my body doesn't want to get moving again. Today, however, should be an easy day. I wait until 11:20 to get the ferry – feeling tired I make mistake of drinking too much coffee and I need to pee no less than five times on the ferry journey, which lasts less than hour. I also make the silly mistake of not eating on the ferry and get hit with a huge hill immediately after disembarking. I have zero energy and I feel hugely unfit. I can't find my rhythm today and I feel sluggish. I don't feel thirsty nor hungry, but, unsurprisingly, when I do eat some food my legs seem to find it a bit easier. I see my first road sign for Bergen which provides a temporary morale boost, but mostly I feel desperate to be off the hot roads and resetting myself ready to go again tomorrow. I never quite snap out of my fogginess and the day passes in a hazy, sweaty blur. I wake up several times in the night feeling anxious and panicking about something I can't put my finger on.

Waking on the penultimate day of the ride, I snooze my alarm for 30 minutes, eventually dragging myself out of my sleeping bag and packing up my tent in slow motion. The weather stays cloudy and overcast all day, which matches my general mood but also makes a welcome change from the sweltering heat. I decide to take the longer route, not wanting to deal with the busy traffic on the E39. I meet three more cyclists at a ferry terminal – one British couple and one German man.

As we sit down together at a table on the ferry, I

discover that the couple have been doing the North Sea cycle route in stages, whereas the German guy has cycled from Munich. All three of us are heading to Bergen to finish but each of has different end destinations for this day. We compare favourite sections, headwind stories and general banter – mostly about peanut butter. The couple has been staying in hotels whilst the German chap has also been camping, and he expresses disbelief that I am also carrying my tent. His set up is much heavier than mine – a fact that makes me feel immensely smug. Compared to bikepacking friends, my set up is usually on the very heavy side, so it's novel to feel like the streamlined version for once.

There is light rain when we get off the ferry, and for the first 15 minutes I am shivering, but I soon warm up thanks to the by now predictably arduous terrain. Steep, sweaty climbs followed by long exhilarating descents characterise the rest of the day. Even overcast and cloudy, Norway is totally stunning. As tired as I am, the sight of two magnificent bridges cheer me up, with their backdrop of dramatic fjords and thick clouds rolling in over the mountains.

I pedal into Stord happily worn out and struggle to stay awake past 7pm. One more day. Just one more day. It feels totally surreal. My energy reserves were drained long ago; I am exhausted and desperate to finish. Although I know I will miss Norway, I am longing to go home; to laugh with friends, to hug my nieces and nephews, to rest.

I paint my nails with a teal coloured nail polish I bought in Sweden on my birthday and have been carrying especially for the final day – the time has at last come. I return from the local supermarket with my usual feast of instant noodles, some token fresh veg (in this case, broccoli and spinach – both of which I can also eat raw throughout the next day), smoked salmon and a milkshake (banana this time), and then set about to also eat whatever food I have left remaining – which happens to include a couple of left-over ready-made pancakes and a tin of pineapple. Feast fit for a queen!

As I have done every night before I ride, I make up tortilla wraps with peanut butter and manuka honey to eat the next day. I polish off the rest of the wraps with more peanut butter and then, not wanting to carry the extra weight but also not wanting to waste any food, I just eat the rest of the peanut butter straight out of the jar by the spoon-ful. I fall asleep soon after eating, happy and with a full belly.

10 TODAY IS YOUR DAY

'YOU'RE OFF TO GREAT PLACES!

Today is your day!
Your mountain is waiting,
So . . . get on your way!'
– Dr Seuss

The morning starts like any other but today is the final day, the day that thousands of miles of cycling has led to. The first song that comes on my playlist is 'Coming Home' by Sigma – which immediately sends me over the edge. I get a lump in my throat as I try, unsuccessfully, to choke back the tears which soon roll down my face. I can't believe this day has finally come. Norway treats me to yet more incredible views – as if purposefully making it hard to leave. I know I will miss Norway and a tinge of sadness knots my stomach that this is my last day. Everything gets new significance – my last ferry, my last Orange Fanta from a petrol station, my last stale sandwich.

I reach a sign that tells me I have 32 kilometres left to Bergen – at which point I promptly burst into uncontrollable, happy tears. Tears that are so violent I have to stop the bike as my whole body heaves with triumphant sobbing. All at once, the significance of the journey hits me. It's the final day. I haven't failed, I will not fail and I am nearly there.

I think of all the times I desperately wanted to quit, all the times I found myself heaped over the handlebars of my bike feeling like this was absolutely impossible and that I'd stupidly bitten off way more than I could chew. I feel overwhelmed with gratitude that I hadn't given up – that I hadn't robbed myself of this electric feeling. I think of proving every critic wrong – and most importantly, proving my own inner gremlin wrong.

The closer I get to Bergen, the more surreal it feels. I expect when I finally do arrive, I will be over emotional and cry all over again. Instead, as I slowly roll into the picturesque city, I feel suddenly calm. A deep, quiet contentment settles over me. I feel peaceful. I rest Dory against a bridge and for a while we both just lean against it, the dark green paint flaked away in some places exposing the metal of the structure underneath. I stare up in wonder at the colourful houses of Bergen and the formidable mountains and ominous clouds that surround them. All around, people are commuting home from work and just carrying on their daily lives, but for Dory and I, this is a day like no other, in a place that we've been dreaming of for months. Seventy days after those first, shaky steps off the ferry into Shetland, here we are. Months of sweat, tears, laughter, desperation and doubt that this moment would ever come – months of striving towards one singular goal of getting here to Bergen: we made it!

As a celebration, I am booked into a proper hotel for the

final two nights before heading back to the UK. I bump into the husband and wife cycling duo I met on the ferry yesterday as I approach the hotel. With my emotions bubbling under the surface but now having a viable outlet, I envelope both of them in an overly zealous and rather sweaty hug, even though they have been here an hour already and have already showered and changed into fresh clothes, so I'm not sure they appreciate it.

As soon as I check into my hotel room, I decide a celebratory dance is in order. 'In the Summer Time' by Mungo Jerry is the first song that comes on and I go all out, using up whatever shreds of energy I had left. Still wearing my stinky lycra, I jump around on the bed, I wiggle my hips, I dip and dive all around the room, while waving my hands around in the air. This, right here, is a happiness that money cannot buy. Unadulterated joy pulses through every cell of my body and I still can't quite believe I'm at the finish line. Everything else, including a shower, is just going to have to wait until the hotel room dance party finishes.

After a shower, I sit down on the bed and get ready to update people with the happy news that this journey is over. I struggle to think of what to say, of how to possibly summarise what this journey has meant to me and how grateful I am to everyone who has followed along with me on social media and provided daily support and encouragement.

Later, amidst all of the congratulations flooding in, it still doesn't seem real – nothing feels different yet. In many ways, today is a day like any other over the past two and a half months. It is only later, when I take off the front bags from Dory that it begins to hit me. The front bags, attached to the handlebars, have not been removed since I started because they were so fiddly to fit precisely on my small bike

frame. As I take them off and get Dory ready to pack up for
the flight home it dawns on me all over again – we did it. For
all my fretting about my mechanical incompetence, we
didn't have a single issue. 'Thanks, baby,' I say, and then I
wrap my arms around her in a long hug. So much more than
a bike, she has been the best teammate I could have asked
for. Never judging my temper tantrums, my tears or my
tendency to sing cheesy pop hits or show tunes at full
volume on an almost daily basis. Always there, right beside
me through it all – trusty, reliable, ever faithful Dory.

That night I struggle to sleep, despite the luxurious bed.
I lie there, tossing and turning; the fancy air conditioning
scratches my throat and thoughts of the impending return to
reality toss and turn around my chaotic head. For nearly
three months, I've led a simple life – eat, cycle, sleep, repeat
– and as I lie there, thinking of all the things that are soon to
start piling up on my To Do list, I feel restless and
exhausted all at once.

The next morning, I have a 10am appointment with the
bike shop, four miles away, to box up Dory ready for our
flight home. I'm there early – routine is routine and I
struggle to hit the road later than 9am. It feels strange to be
riding her there knowing I will not be riding her back.
Without any weight on the bike, the occasional hill is easy
now and we gently cruise along, mostly freewheeling,
savouring the final few moments of movement in Norway
together before this chapter comes to its inevitable close.

I get hit with an irrational pang of anxiety as they wheel
Dory out of sight – feeling like a worried relative watching
her loved one getting taken into surgery. When she comes
back, dismantled and contorted to fit into the large card-
board bike box, I feel all at odds having lost my aluminium
ally. It's a short taxi ride back to the hotel – the speed of

travelling in a car now feeling incredibly fast and alien after travelling so much slower for so long. Rather guiltily, I feel a little thankful to be in the car going up each and every single hill – my legs twitch in fresh memory of the burn that this terrain brings.

The next mission is to pick up a cheap suitcase to pack my kit and panniers into for the flight home. Before that, I first need to drop Dory back off at the hotel. I awkwardly tumble with her and the gigantic box into the lift and ungracefully shuffle her along the corridor to my room. I then head straight back out into Bergen to begin the search. I soon find myself in a huge shopping centre, with a labyrinth of escalators that I find overwhelming and confusing. I can see the floor that I need to get to but somehow I always seem to be at the wrong end for the escalator that takes me there. Navigating across whole countries was much easier than this. Eventually, I make it, and feeling flustered by the whole process, purchase the first case I find and noisily wheel it along the cobbled streets back to the hotel once more.

Back in the room, I take a look at the chaotic scene before me – lycra, spare inner tubes, helmet, shoes, tent, sleeping bag and more lycra all spread out and hanging from various surfaces in the room, as if thrown around by some kind of deranged and terribly angry octopus. Why is there a vest on the lampshade? Why are my shorts hanging over the TV? I'm not quite ready to tackle any of it yet so I promptly leave the hotel room for the third time that day and head out in search of pizza instead. I slowly amble around Bergen, soaking up every final moment of this journey before the early morning flight the next day.

I struggle to sleep again that night. My daily rhythm is all at odds and my mind whirls with all the things that await when I get home – all the things I need to organise and all the people to see. The next morning, as I've now come to expect from the Norwegians, my taxi driver is incredibly friendly and has a few adventurous tales of his own hidden up his sleeve. We exchange travel tales and laugh as we roll through the quiet early morning light – his smile only once turning into a stern frown when I mention the 'tunnels of doom' day, and he quickly confirms my fear of just how many cyclists have lost their lives in those tunnels. I promise him I won't ever do it again.

Waiting to board my flight home, I'm torn between excitement for seeing all the people I've missed and wanting to relocate to Norway. My heart swells with love and gratitude when I think of all the Norwegian people that made me feel so welcome, so safe and so understood. I think of how Norway's brutal terrain pushed me to breaking point but then rewarded me with breathtaking views that made it all so worthwhile. It was, without doubt, worth every pedal stroke to get there. As the plane rises into the sky, I look out of the window and watch the monumental terrain of Norway get ever smaller. I think of London – the hectic, dirty city I'm headed back to – and my heart sinks a little.

Arriving back to London Heathrow, a rush of stifling and oppressive heat greets me as soon as I step off the plane. The airport is rammed full of people, all of them seemingly in an urgent rush and incredibly offended by my bike box; they repeatedly scowl at me when they accidentally ram themselves into it when trying to overtake me at speed.

My oldest brother, Simon, is picking me up but is running late. Simon is nearly always late – reliably and predictably so – but we love him very much anyway. 'Simon time' ranges from 30–90 minutes later than whatever time zone you find yourself in with him. The familiarity of this dynamic makes me smile. With time to kill, I decide to treat myself to a snack from a vending machine – which promptly takes my money and doesn't give me my snack. Out of principle, I then spend five minutes on the overpriced helpline to get my money back. Oh, England. Inefficient, rude and so very stinky in this uncharacteristic heat – I've missed you.

When Simon does arrive, he gives me a huge brotherly hug and then we get lost around the car park of Heathrow for several minutes before eventually escaping. Navigating modern infrastructures is clearly not a strong Kennington trait.

On my first few days back home, I am overwhelmed with appreciation for all the mundane things:

Limitless cups of tea (even though we're in a heat wave)

Clean clothes (clothes to choose from!) and no more rationing of clean underwear and trying to decide which is the 'lucky' day I get to wear clean pants

A hot shower

More tea

Being able to just pop to the loo whenever I like, not having to scout out a bush, ditch or a petrol station

My own bed. Not having to hunt for a place to sleep!

That first night back I sleep for ten hours straight. I feel thankful that I don't have to pack up my bags, like I have almost every night for the past 74 days. Science tells us that it takes 30 days to form a new habit. It feels utterly surreal to be out of the rhythm of life on the road.

As I re-adjust to life back home, I feel a deep sense of contentment, better than any fleeting euphoria I've felt from smaller challenges. I feel like I've caught up to where I want to be. For once, I feel like I have done enough. I gave that ride everything I had – physically, emotionally and mentally it took so much more to complete it than I ever knew I had. I finished it knowing I did my best and that I emptied out the tank, more than once. I'm blissfully exhausted and at peace; I feel this unique sensation of happiness with exactly where I am. I have been chasing this moment for years, over thousands of miles and across rivers, roads and oceans. I know there are so many more adventures still to come but for now, it feels good to be home.

EPILOGUE

*'Have the heart of a giant, but know you're a man
...Start small, grow tall'*
– 'Little Giant' by Roo Panes

W hen I first started exploring endurance adventures, I decided to label all of my endeavours under a code name: Project Kairos. I discovered the ancient Greek word *kairos* in 2014 and immediately knew I'd found something that described adventure and indeed life perfectly for me.

'KAIROS: The right or opportune moment (the supreme moment); a time lapse, a moment of indeterminate time in which everything happens.

The perfect, delicate, crucial moment; the fleeting rightness of time and place that creates the opportune atmosphere for action, words, or movement.'

. . .

PROJECT KAIROS WAS BORN when I realised the right time to follow that dream is right now – you just need to seize it.

A couple of months after coming back from Norway, following a busy series of talks all over the UK, I found myself at St James's Palace, by special invitation of HRH Prince Edward, Earl of Wessex, to celebrate the Gold Duke of Edinburgh Awards. Assembled there were hundreds of young adults who had recently completed their Gold award and I was there to deliver a short inspiring talk as part of the awards ceremony. As I stood up in front of hundreds of those impeccably dressed and slightly nervous young adults and their very proud guests, I looked around at the regal setting – the elaborate gold leaf decorations, the royal portraits and the plush carpets – and internally I smiled at how far I'd come. Who would have thought that initial leap from a cliff in America would one day lead to a royal palace in London?

I spoke about what it means to me to lead a courageous life, and how adventures have taught me to nourish that spark of possibility, no matter how small it may seem – sometimes a spark is all you need. It was the butterflies in my stomach that led me to take a literal leap of faith from that cliff and I'd learnt to trust them ever since.

Endurance adventures have taught me resilience and inner strength; they have taught me when to walk away, when to shut out the critics and when to defiantly stand my ground. Although many people have concerns about the safety of travelling solo as a female, my self-propelled journeys have shown me that, for the most part, this world is overflowing with kindness - and is not something to be feared. I have learnt that it's OK to fail sometimes, as long as I did my best. In fact, where there is no risk of failure there is also no room for growth. I have also learnt the importance of saying no to the things that don't matter, so that I'm able to say yes to the things that do.

Building a career in adventure has taught me to own my space in this world. The lessons learnt to survive tough times on the road, in the sea or on the river have helped me survive tough times in life, too. Resilience is a muscle that gets stronger the more you use it.

I often think of the harrowing tale of how elephants are trained in the circus. Baby elephants are tied by rope to a wooden post planted deep in the ground. At first, these infant elephants will try to snap the rope, to break free and to explore further. However, try as they might, they cannot escape the restraint. This is repeated daily until eventually the elephants learn that their attempts to break the rope is futile. When they do eventually grow up into majestic adults, some five tons in weight and could easily snap the rope, they don't even try. The image of a magnificent giant elephant confined by a puny little rope breaks my heart (as does the circus in general, but that's a discussion for another time) and I see a similar pattern in humans every day. Whatever our own ropes are made from – past failures, lack of confidence or societal pressure – we stay bound, not realising how strong we really are.

I'm not here to berate people who work Monday to Friday, or suggest that everyone who reads this book should quit their jobs to become a full-time adventurer – but I do believe in a life full of purpose, whatever that means to you. Considering how much of your life will be spent at work, isn't it worth putting some thought into what that looks like?

I consider 'Follow your passion' to be fairly terrible

advice because it oversimplifies and over-romanticises the process of finding a satisfying career. However, I do think that finding something you're passionate about, and therefore don't mind working hard at, is a very worthy endeavour. I didn't build or monetise my career in adventure overnight, but I figured that the time was going to pass anyway, so I might as well let it pass whilst at least striving towards doing something I loved – even if only part time at first.

Small steps with intention add up and I think that perseverance is a superpower – but nothing changes if nothing changes. No innovation ever came from playing it safe. Honestly, what's the worst that could happen? I think that asking better questions in general is important for a better life. One of my favourite questions to repeatedly ask of myself is: 'What am I capable of?' We often sell ourselves short but that's such a powerful question to ask if you demand an honest answer from yourself.

Adventure, success and happiness are terms that mean something different to everyone and I think they inevitably mean different things to us all at various stages in life, too. However, if there's one thing I know for certain, it's that it's worth nourishing that spark.

A wise man, John Augustus Shedd, once said, 'A ship in harbor is safe, but that is not what ships are built for.' I think it's the same with humans. Modern life is so comfortable, predictable and safe that many of us have forgotten the incredible potential that lies within each and every one of us. The only way you will find out what you're capable of is if you dare to explore your limits, and I'm certain you will surprise yourself and discover new depths of brilliant ability when you really try. I have learnt to love, respect and admire the human body for the phenomenal things it can do, not just what it looks like. We are built for so much more.

Kairos. Be brave. Take the leap.

AUTHOR'S NOTE

I really hope that you have enjoyed reading this book and you've had fun adventuring vicariously with me through these pages. I would be forever grateful if you could take a moment to leave a review on Amazon - no matter how brief! As an independently published Author, each and every review is hugely important to me and it really helps this book reach more people. Hooray!

To stay in the loop about future books, adventures and other fun antics - connect with me on social media:

Facebook: 'Laura Kairos'
Instagram: @LauraKairos
Twitter: @KairosLaura

Alternatively, digital basecamp (aka my website) is www.lauraexplorer.com.

THANK YOU'S

Hero, thy name is Mum (or, Carrie McHale to others).
Thank you for relentlessly cheering in my corner, for the
sacrifices you've made, for the endless cups of tea and countless hours of wise counsel that usually come with them, for
being adamantly optimistic at all times, for letting me intermittently turn your office into my bedroom and for always
encouraging me to dream big. This wouldn't have been
possible without you.

To Dad, for offering constant encouragement, support and
much needed humour - usually all at the same time.

To my elder brothers Simon and Rhys for always having my
back.

To my younger (but ridiculously tall) brother Kai. Thanks
for always being ready with a giant-sized hug and a silly
joke to make me smile.

To Dave Cornthwaite for your valuable advice, constant encouragement, precious friendship, wonderful hugs and terrible accents.

To Sean Conway for answering my many, many questions over the years about self-publishing, endurance swimming, documentary proposals and everything else in between.

To Louise Coulcher - aka Weeze. For being the first reader and editor of this book, for being a loyal best friend, for gently nudging me away from bad life decisions and for always rooting for me. Bear. Force. Gratitude.

To Siobhan Alt. Thanks for always being there over the years with a hug and a slice of cake - and for being the best friend a girl (or granny) could ask for.

To Tessa Jennett, Kate Davis and Elise Downing. For all of the joy and hilarity our friendship brings into my life. Thanks for helping me get through the considerably less cheerful moments, too.

To Rob and Ed Underwood. For being my go-to creative solution finders. With extra thanks to Ed for being my road trip/logistics buddy and all round excellent friend.

To Mark "Ironmate" Kleanthous and Clare Kleanthous. Thanks for always enthusiastically supporting every crazy idea I mention to you and for never failing to be a beacon of encouragement.

To Liz Marvin - editor extraordinaire. Thanks for adding your magic touch to these pages. I can't imagine this book without your amazing input

To Raphael Rychetsky. Thank you for enduring hours of driving and putting up with the midges of Scotland in order to take the cover photo for this book.

To Maren Tönnies and the rest of the team at KEEN Footwear. Thank you for giving me the opportunity to grow with you as an ambassador, for always believing in my potential and for your constant support with all that I do.

To the team at BAM Bamboo Clothing. Thank you for adopting me as an ambassador all those years ago and thank you for keeping me cosy ever since.

To Anthony Goddard at ZeroSixZero - the almighty map Wizard! Thanks for helping me share my journeys and for always having a hilarious story (or 3) ready at all times.

To all the sponsors that not only make my adventures possible but also support and encourage me throughout the year: Aethic, DryRobe, Mark Brigham at Ellis Brigham Mountain Sports, Dan Graham and Sam Gregory at F45 Stratford, Osprey Europe and PowerTraveller.

Lastly but most definitely not least... Thank you to YOU (yes, YOU!) reading this. My trips are often solo but are very much a team effort. I'm very grateful to everyone who has supported my adventures from afar via social media.. Many of you have offered words of encouragement when I've needed them the most, some of you have shown up in person (usually with chocolate, you heroes!) and your kindness and enthusiasm over the years makes this all possible. I love sharing my stories with you all - thank you for listening, for inspiring me and cheering me on. Here's to many more!

It's inevitable that I've missed some people off this list - if that is you, I'm sorry. For everyone who's played a part, no matter how small, in supporting me - thank you!

ENDORSEMENTS FOR LAURA KENNINGTON: SPEAKER

"This was 15 minutes of high octane inspiration which had our attendees racing to put on their cycling gear. Laura's talk was TED quality with down-to-earth advice and added storytelling flair. Plus some bloody good music. If you're looking for a motivational speaker for your next event, you've found her." — **Kim Willis, The Heroine's Journey Speaker Series**

"You were the best guest speaker we've had! Your talk was very inspiring and engaged so many people. I had many members of staff come up to me to say how interesting your story was." — **Emma Belsey, The Folkestone Academy**

"Laura, you were brilliant. A bonafide dance like-you-are-alive enabler! If you need someone to make a full marquee of people fully dance, this is your woman." — **MJ Kinnear, Yestival**

"Laura is a great speaker who inspired our audience of young people and parents. Her engaging personality, humour and stories of determination and strength was an inspiration – she interacted with the audience well and has a perfect personality for talking. I hope we will be able to use Laura again." — **Greg Stewart, District Commissioner Bishops Stortford Scouts**

"Listening to Laura Kennington speak is good for your soul." — **Rima Patel, Yes Stories: A Night of Inspiration**

"If you want your pupils to really understand what embracing life's opportunities is all about get Laura to come and talk to your school.The stories of her adventures were both fun and inspiring and I challenge anyone who hears her speak not to be motivated to undertake some kind of challenge as a result – no matter how small." — **Toby Batchelor, Cranleigh Prep School**

Find out more about Laura's speaking via her website: www.lauraexplorer.com
Or email: hello@lauraexplorer.com

ABOUT THE AUTHOR

Laura Kennington is a British endurance athlete, adventurer and professional speaker with a passion for the endurance capability of the human body (and also a passion for ice cream).

Laura spent her early years as the only female sibling on a farm in Bury St Edmunds, Suffolk. She discovered adventure at an early age by embracing muddy countryside exploration with the beloved family dog, Hobo, a White Alsation.

As an adult, her adventures include solo kayaking a section of the Volga river in Russia, solo cycling the world's longest coastal route in Ireland, solo cycling Scotland's North Coast 500 route, running the length of Fuerteventura (100 miles) in 4 days and circumnavigating three of the Channel Islands using three different sporting disciplines as part of a rather extreme triathlon! She has most recently returned from solo cycling 3700 miles along the North Sea-facing coasts of 8 countries, from Scotland to Norway!

A strong believer in the positive impact that adventure and sport can have on children and adults alike, Laura uses her human powered journeys as a platform to inspire and encourage others to get outside.

Ingram Content Group UK Ltd.
Milton Keynes UK
UKHW012050140423
420194UK00006B/502